Global Financial Markets series

Global Financial Markets is a series of practical guides to the latest financial market tools, techniques and strategies. Written for practitioners across a range of disciplines it provides comprehensive but practical coverage of key topics in finance covering strategy, markets, financial products, tools and techniques and their implementation. This series will appeal to a broad readership, from new entrants to experienced practitioners across the financial services industry, including areas such as institutional investment; financial derivatives; investment strategy; private banking; risk management; corporate finance and M&A, financial accounting and governance, and many more.

Titles include:

Guy Fraser-Sampson
INTELLIGENT INVESTING
A Guide to the Practical and Behavioural Aspects of Investment Strategy

Michael Hünseler
CREDIT PORTFOLIO MANAGEMENT
A Practitioner's Guide to the Active Management of Credit Risks

Gianluca Oricchio
PRIVATE COMPANY VALUATION
How Credit Risk Reshaped Equity Markets and Corporate Finance Valuation Tools

Global Financial Markets series
Series Standing Order ISBN 978–1–137–32734–5

You can receive future titles in this series as they are published by placing a standing order. Please contact your bookseller or, in case of difficulty, write to us at the address below with your name and address, the title of the series and the ISBN quoted above.

Customer Services Department, Macmillan Distribution Ltd, Houndmills, Basingstoke, Hampshire RG21 6XS, England, UK

Also by Guy Fraser-Sampson

MULTI-ASSET CLASS INVESTMENT STRATEGY

PRIVATE EQUITY AS AN ASSET CLASS (Second Edition)

ALTERNATIVE ASSETS: Investments for a Post-Crisis World

NO FEAR FINANCE: An Introduction to Finance and Investment for the Non-Finance Professional

THE MESS WE'RE IN: Why Politicians Can't Fix Financial Crises

Intelligent Investing

A Guide to the Practical and Behavioural Aspects of Investment Strategy

Guy Fraser-Sampson

First published 2013 by
PALGRAVE MACMILLAN

Palgrave Macmillan in the UK is an imprint of Macmillan Publishers Limited, registered in England, company number 785998, of Houndmills, Basingstoke, Hampshire RG21 6XS.

Palgrave Macmillan in the US is a division of St Martin's Press LLC, 175 Fifth Avenue, New York, NY 10010.

Palgrave Macmillan is the global academic imprint of the above companies and has companies and representatives throughout the world.

Palgrave® and Macmillan® are registered trademarks in the United States, the United Kingdom, Europe and other countries

ISBN 978–1–137–26408–4

This book is printed on paper suitable for recycling and made from fully managed and sustained forest sources. Logging, pulping and manufacturing processes are expected to conform to the environmental regulations of the country of origin.

A catalogue record for this book is available from the British Library.

A catalog record for this book is available from the Library of Congress.

Contents

List of Figures

1
What Is Strategy?

This is a book about investment strategy (the title being a bit of a giveaway). It will set out the way in which investors of all types and sizes can work towards identifying and implementing the approach to investment that is most likely to achieve their objectives. As will be seen, this process is infinitely more complex than might at first be thought.

The good news, however, is that it is complex rather than complicated. There is no individual part of the process that is inherently difficult in itself. However, the number of different issues which must be considered, not just individually but also in terms of how they affect and interact with all the others, does present a very real challenge.

That challenge is made all the more daunting by two aspects of the way in which we think. First, we have no experience of thinking strategically during our normal working lives, which are taken up with operational decisions relevant to our day-to-day responsibilities. Second, when we learn about finance and investment they are invariably presented to us as a science, most likely some form of mathematics, and thus we tend to approach investment matters by trying to apply the sort of rigorously objective and quantitative approach demanded by science in order to find the 'one right answer'. Asset allocation models, commonly called 'Optimisers' are good examples of this. As we shall see, however, the strategic process requires a completely different mind-set. Quantitative techniques, for example, are a necessary part of the process, but only a part, and they only take us so far.

More fundamentally, the process is often undone by people not actually understanding just what 'strategy' is, which at best leads to them skipping an entire (and vital) stage of analysis, and at worst renders the whole exercise largely meaningless. This, then, must be our starting point.

In part, the confusion arises because the terms 'strategy' and 'tactics' are often, rather sloppily, used interchangeably in everyday speech when in fact they have quite different meanings and applications. This difference is well appreciated in the field of military affairs, within which much work on strategy has been published, and so perhaps we may begin our discussion of strategy by distinguishing between the three different levels at which thinking and planning should take place: strategic, tactical and operational. We might illustrate this by using as an example the Second Battle of El Alamein in 1942.

The situation at this time was that the German and Italian forces, under German Field Marshal Erwin Rommel, had fought their way to the boundaries of Egypt in a series of brilliant manoeuvres, aided and abetted by some very indifferent generalship on the part of the Allied forces. Recognising these shortcomings almost too late, the Allied Commander-in-Chief, Sir Claude Auchinleck, had dismissed his army commander and taken personal control of proceedings. Snatching victory from the jaws of defeat, he halted Rommel at the First Battle of El Alamein. Most commentators now recognise that this marked the turning point of the desert war. Rommel was left too weakened to dislodge the Allies from their defensive positions, and could not bypass them without being struck in the rear and flank if he did so; Auchinleck had in fact already attempted to do this as the battle drew to a close, but had been let down by his subordinate commanders, who had developed the habit under his predecessor of treating orders as voluntary guidelines.

Auchinleck none the less realised that Rommel's stubborn persistence would not let him admit that the game was now over without at least one more roll of the dice, and so he prepared to fight another defensive battle along the ridges protecting his position to the south. However, at this juncture, Auchinleck was abruptly sacked by Prime Minister Winston Churchill for political reasons. He was replaced as Commander-in-Chief by Field Marshal Harold Alexander, and as army commander by Lieutenant-General William Gott, yet another highly questionable decision by Churchill, since Gott as a corps commander had been one of the prime offenders during recent months when it came to disregarding orders. However, Gott was killed in a plane crash while flying to take up his command, and so it was Bernard Montgomery, the future Field Marshal, who was to fight what became known as the Battle of Alam el Halfa, using Auchinleck's plan and his dispositions, as Rommel made his final forlorn attempt to break through. Finally recognising defeat, Rommel settled into prepared defensive positions opposite the allies at El Alamein before departing for medical treatment in Germany. Thus the initiative had shifted decisively to the Allies, especially as they were supplied with substantial reinforcements, including two entire armoured divisions, and hence enjoyed a considerable numerical advantage.

Let us first examine the strategic issues that now faced Alexander and Montgomery. Strategy relates to the big picture. Because it is the starting point, it is vital that we begin at the very top of the pyramid of issues and decisions. We must identify those things that are fundamental, that operate upon other things, but which are not themselves operated on by anything but themselves. In military terms this translates into 'How can we best win the war?'.

It is in fact very rare for generals to have to address truly strategic issues in a battlefield context. Such decisions are usually taken by ministers and defence chiefs in solemn conference some time previously, and at a distance. That is what makes the Second Battle of El Alamein so interesting, and such a useful example.

You see, what Alexander and Montgomery knew was that Winston Churchill and the US President Franklin D. Roosevelt had agreed to launch Operation Torch, the invasion of North Africa from the west, and that these attacks would be taking place a few weeks hence. When they did, the Axis forces opposite El Alamein would be forced into a lengthy and hasty retreat as they scrambled to link up with their counterparts in the west before the Allied forces could get between them and cut their supply lines. Thus, in addressing the strategic question of 'How can we best win the war?' they had a very fundamental decision to make: should they actually fight the battle at all? Would launching an attack contribute anything significant to winning the war, or would it be more sensible to hold all their mobile forces, and particularly their tanks, ready to pursue the enemy as it withdrew, and, it was hoped, to destroy its forces (or at the very least inflict significant losses and dislocation) as they did so?

With the benefit of hindsight it is easy to see that Alexander and Montgomery made the wrong decision. The Allies were to suffer more than 13,000 casualties, would at various times come close to losing (or at least failing to win) the battle despite their overwhelming superiority, and even after it was over, timid generalship by Montgomery would allow the Axis forces, once again under the command of Rommel, recalled from his sickbed, to slip away to the west after all, albeit being only a shadow of their former selves.

This is a classic example of emotion and politics being allowed to interfere with the rational process, something which, alas, happens in business and finance all the time. Montgomery wanted his battle to prove his credentials as a general, and prove he was superior to Auchinleck (though, ironically, if anything it did the opposite, though this was not recognised at the time). There is also a sense that the British realised, from Torch onwards, that they would be the junior partners in the alliance, and that this represented the last chance for a 'British' (in fact largely Indian, Australian, New Zealand and South African) army to show that it could inflict a decisive defeat on the German forces. Again, ironically, it would prove to be a technical victory but a moral defeat; with their superiority in men and equipment, and enjoying total control of the air, the 'British' should have won easily, and on schedule.

This, then, is the strategic level. As we shall see, it is driven by big, fundamental questions such as 'Who are we?' and 'What are we trying to achieve?'

One level down from this come tactical considerations, which might be characterised by the question: 'How do we win this battle?'. Viewed in this way, the difference between strategy and tactics, and the danger of confusing the two, will, it is to be hoped, be obvious. Yet it is a common confusion; in my experience most investors largely ignore the strategic level and go straight to tactics. Because of this they are, of course, holding their discussions in a vacuum. Tactics are supposed to be the means of implementing a discussed and agreed strategy. On their own, they are largely irrelevant; they are a means, not an end.

The management writer, Peter Drucker,[1] summed this up perfectly when he pointed out that it is far more important to do the right thing (even if done imperfectly) than to do things in the right way. Doing the wrong thing well and energetically can be disastrous. Drucker reinforced the distinction by urging us to think about strategy as 'effectiveness', and tactics as 'efficiency'. Strategy is about choosing the optimum (most effective) course of action. Tactics is about how well (efficiently) we execute it.

At the Second Battle of El Alamein, Montgomery had a choice between making a broad flanking manoeuvre out into the desert to try to avoid the Axis fixed defences and to find a way round them to the south, or to attack them frontally. He chose the latter, partly because his temperament required him to fight a tightly controlled battle, but perhaps partly because he was unfamiliar, and thus uncomfortable, with the wide expanses of the desert after his experience of the relatively confined battlefields of Northern Europe, and partly because he lacked confidence (with some justification, given their recent history) in his subordinate commanders to follow orders.

His tactics chosen, he then had to decide how best to implement these on the ground, at the level of the individual unit. This is what is called the

---

1. Peter F. Drucker, *The Effective Executive*, New York: Butterworth-Heinemann, 2007.

operational level, and these decisions are often left to subordinate commanders, but Montgomery wanted to control every aspect of the battle, and therefore laid down very carefully what was to happen, even briefing individual battalion commanders personally.

In this case, the Axis defences were protected by deep minefields, which were in turn covered by anti-tank guns. Montgomery therefore directed that the infantry (since there were not nearly enough engineers to do the job on their own) should clear narrow lanes through the minefields for the tanks to use. This was done by the simple, though highly dangerous, expedient of walking slowly ahead (while being shot at), and poking the ground with a bayonet. The fact that troops in Afghanistan had to resort to an identical procedure some 70 years later is a sad comment on the ongoing failure of the British army to supply its men with the right tools for the job.[2]

So there we have the three levels of decision-making: strategic, tactical and operational. Clearly, they are listed in declining order of importance. Getting your infantry platoon moving ahead smartly will not be much use if you are advancing towards the strongest, rather than the weakest, part of the enemy line. Similarly, even if your battle plan is a model of intellectual rigour, it will not help you if, while you are busy winning this battle, a different enemy force is cutting off your communications and supplies. Nor if your leaders are ordering large parts of your forces off to different theatres of war (as happened with some of Montgomery's predecessors), so that you will be unable to follow up your victory even if you achieve it.

The levels of decision-making are also stated in declining order of their easiness to change. If your platoon is pinned down by an enemy machine gun, it is a relatively simple matter to send half a dozen men off to outflank it while the rest provide covering fire. If you decide that a whole division is attacking in the wrong place, it can take several days (as it did at El Alamein) to move it and all its support echelons from one location to another. Trying to change your strategy in midstream (as the British and French did when they dithered over invading Norway in 1940) leads to whole shiploads of troops and supplies being, loaded, unloaded, reloaded and re-routed. Ensuing disaster, as in that case, is usually both predictable and inevitable. As another management guru, Michael Porter,[3] said: 'strategy must have continuity; it can't be constantly reinvented'.

---

2. This 'BARMA-ing', as it became known in Afghanistan, should in any event have been unnecessary had the Government supplied the troops with helicopters so they did not have to travel on the ground, as happened with their American counterparts.

3. Keith M. Hammond, 'Michael Porter's Big Ideas', available at www.fastcompany. com.

It follows, then, that strategic decisions have far more impact than tactical ones on resulting events, even though they may seem to be more remote from the decision. There is research that purports to show this. A 1991 study,[4] following from an earlier one undertaken in 1986, found that asset allocation (strategic) decisions accounted for over 90 per cent of investor outperformance when compared with manager selection (tactical) decisions. Note the word 'purports'. This study has been rightly criticised for ignoring the effect of management fees. It is also only fair to point out that the asset types considered were a fairly narrow selection, as was customary at the time. Its methodology in calculating returns has also been queried.[5]

However, while the extent to which the outcomes of strategic decisions outweigh those of tactical decisions may be open to question, the general principle is not. A peer-reviewed academic paper published in 2000,[6] which looked at mutual funds rather than pension funds (as the 1991 one had done), broadly supports this, while refining the questions asked. It finds that effectively 100% of an individual fund's outperformance may be ascribed to strategic asset allocation (using what the study calls 'the policy return'). However, when it comes to comparing any one fund with any other as an external observer, such as a financial analyst seeking to choose between them, asset allocation explained about 40 per cent of the variation in returns. Whatever the case, it seems clear that, for investors, it is asking the right strategic questions, and answering them correctly, that will account for most, if not all, investment outperformance.

All of which strongly suggests that any investment decision-making body, such as the investment committee or board of trustees of a pension fund, should spend at least 90 per cent of their time discussing strategic issues (choosing the right asset types) rather than tactical issues (choosing the right managers). After all, if you have chosen the wrong asset type in the first place, then what difference does it make if you happen to choose one or two managers who may outperform against their peers within that mistakenly chosen asset class? Drucker says that doing the wrong thing very efficiently is frequently worse than doing nothing at all – and academic studies support him. They show that choosing the right asset types may account for almost all of outperformance, whereas

4. Brinson, Gary P., Singer, Brian D., Beebower, Gilbert L., 'Determinants of Portfolio Performance II: An Update', *Financial Analysts' Journal*, vol. 47, no.3 (1991).
5. William Jahnke, 'The Asset Allocation Hoax', *Journal of Financial Planning*, February 1997.
6. Roger Ibbotson and Paul Kaplan, 'Does Asset Allocation Policy Explain 100%, 90% or 40% of Performance?', *Financial Analysts' Journal*, vol. 56, no.1 (2000).

choosing the right managers (particularly within the wrong asset type) may account for almost none.

Yet any one who has attended the meetings of such a body will know that in fact the opposite is true. Whole meetings can pass without a single strategic issue being raised, with the attendees proceeding robotically through a fixed and packed agenda, quizzing managers on past performance, and asking consultants for ever more complicated analyses of it, all incidentally based on the fundamental and unquestioned assumption that the future will simply be a repeat showing of the past for those who were unlucky enough to miss out on it the first time round.

For those who glimpse the true significance of the bigger picture, such meetings are at best tedious, and at worst futile and frustrating. Yes, choosing the right managers can make an enormous difference in some areas, such as private equity, but only if you have first chosen the right asset types, and made sensible allocations to each. These asset allocation decisions can only properly be the output of the strategic process, and the fact that so many investors get them wrong is usually because they have never attempted the process at all, but simply chosen them on some random and arbitrary basis.

If you are someone who attends such meetings, then you can easily test this for yourself. Simply ask 'Why?' every time someone makes a statement. If a strategic process has been undergone successfully, then those running the meeting will have a ready and rational answer on each occasion.

Strategy	Tactics
Influences lower level (tactical) decisions, but can itself only be influenced by external factors and changing circumstances	Influences lower level (operational) decisions, but is itself designed to implement higher level (strategic) decisions
Big Picture: How can we win the war?	More specific: How can we win this battle?
Doing the right thing (Drucker)	Doing things right (Drucker)
Effectiveness (Drucker)	Efficiency (Drucker)
Making the right asset allocations	Choosing the right managers
Produces 90–100% of outperformance across a whole fund (academic studies)	Produces 0–10% of outperformance across a whole fund (academic studies)
Vital to succeed. Fatal if you fail	Good to have. Failure will impact adversely on performance to some extent

Figure 1.1 Strategy and tactics

What of the third level, the operational? Well, if strategic decisions are about which are the right assets to hold, and tactical ones about which managers to choose (these are deliberate simplifications at this stage – as we progress you will see that there is much more to it than this), it follows that everything below this must belong to the operational sphere. In front office terms this will mean conducting due diligence on proposed investments and managers; the monitoring of existing investments and managers; and, if appropriate, rebalancing between asset types. In back office terms, it will involve the transfer of funds, accounting for these, and supervisory oversight to ensure compliance with both internal procedures and external regulations. Depending on how your investment process is organised, it might also entail custodianship and brokerage arrangements, as well as all the data entry surrounding the managers reporting to you, and you in turn reporting to your board or committee.

Of course, where these activities – such as due diligence and monitoring – result in manager selection or de-selection decisions, or go/no-go decisions on direct investments, then it is easy to allow everything to start blurring together, but this should not conceal the essentially different nature of these activities. Rarely will those who undertake due diligence also have the authority to make an investment decision based on it (though they may participate in the discussion).

It is also important to understand one basic difference in the way in which the top two levels interact, compared to the bottom two. In both cases there is (or should be) a feedback loop, but this works slightly differently in each case. Where a strategic decision has been made (for example, to allocate 15 per cent to real estate), it may subsequently prove impossible to implement this effectively, in which case the issue will loop back to those who determine strategy to see if they wish to change their minds. Of course, this should not happen, except where circumstances such as market conditions have changed unexpectedly, since the ability to execute on a strategy should have been fully considered when it was set, but happen it does.

In the case of some operational matters, these can be undertaken to allow, or at least to facilitate, the making of tactical decisions. For example, a tactical decision may be taken to favour a particular manager in principle, but detailed due diligence may then be required to decide whether to actually go ahead and appoint that person. It will be comparatively rare for a tactical decision to prove impossible (rather than merely unwise) to execute, and when this does occur it normally does so as a result of internal systems, whether accounting or IT, proving unequal to the challenge.

Of course, in practice, particularly in small organisations such as thinly staffed pension funds, there may be a considerable cross-over in terms of who makes which decisions, and this inevitably makes it more difficult to keep the three levels strictly separate in one's mind, but no matter how difficult this might be, or how artificial it might seem, it is essential to do so. Conducting the strategic process is difficult enough to start with, but once irrelevant or inappropriate issues are allowed to crowd in, it rapidly becomes downright impossible.

Perhaps this is another reason why the strategic and the tactical tend to get confused in practice. If the same people are responsible for both, then there is a temptation simply to start with the existing investment process (tactical/operational) and discuss how this might be improved, rather than asking more fundamental (strategic) questions, such as in which types of assets the organisation should be investing, and why.

Remember that little word, by the way. 'Why?' is the most useful weapon in our strategic armoury. It is our equivalent of Cartesian doubt. By asking it repeatedly we strip away layer after layer of assumptions and conclusions until we get down to the real starting point. Unfortunately for those who are involved on the operational side of things, there seems to be an inbuilt readiness to start with the 'how?' and the 'what?', but these should form part of the output, not the input.

Always bear in mind the objective of investment strategy, which is to arrive at the optimum mix of assets for any single individual investor – 'optimum' in the sense that it is what is most likely to achieve their desired outcome. So, asset allocation should mark the finishing line of the process, not the beginning, as it frequently seems to do in practice.

Why an 'individual' investor? Because no two investors are likely to have exactly the same desired outcome, or at least should not have if they have conducted their process properly, and so it will be almost impossible for exactly the same mix of assets to be optimum for both. Look out for asset mixes that are suspiciously similar to those of other investors, particularly if they are of the same type and geography. Ditto peer benchmarking, where an investor simply adopts as a target rate of return what is aspired to by supposedly similar investors (in reality, simply those with the same label on the tin). Both of these are usually clear indicators that the strategic process has failed, or never even taken place.

It is the need to fix on a desired outcome that drives the whole process, and will, one hopes, prompt thinking that helps to define an organisation's view of itself. 'What are we trying to achieve, and why?' should be a constant companion to the strategic discussion. Staggeringly, this question is rarely asked by boards or investment committees, and even when it is, it tends to be pursued in isolation rather than as the starting point for a wider strategic analysis. Michael Porter again: 'sound strategy starts with [having identified] the right goal'. Incidentally, little in history is new, and certainly little to do with strategy. Writing in the first century AD, the Roman thinker and politician Seneca said that if a sailor does not know which port he is making for, he is unlikely to find a favourable wind.

Knowing your destination is one thing. Most of us can find a large town on a map. Much more difficult is being dropped in open country-side from a closed truck with a map and a compass, and trying to work out your current location. As we shall see, it is just as important to iden-tify the starting point of your journey as it is to know in which direction you are headed. Many recently parachuted secret agents on both sides were caught out during the Second World War by being unable to point to their location on a map when questioned. Similarly, any attempt to set investment strategy without first working out exactly where you stand to begin with is doomed to failure. Yet this is all too common an omission, not least because the emotional need to conform to the conventional wis-dom within the organisation is nowhere stronger than in actually consid-ering the organisation itself.

So, everything we have learnt so far could be summed up by the phrase 'strategy is important' or 'strategy matters'. Yet this does not really go far enough. Strategy is more than important. It is vital and fundamental. None of us would set out on a car journey without first deciding where we wanted to go, considering how to get there, and whether we have enough fuel in the tank. Yet these basic questions are exactly what most of the world's investors neglect. Instead, they set out on an aimless tour of the surrounding countryside, choosing their turns at random, and trusting to luck not to run out of petrol along the way. Without wishing to be cynical, there is, of course, one advantage to all of this if viewed from a certain angle. If you have not actually committed yourself to any definite destination or time of arrival, then you cannot be said to have had an unsuccessful journey, regardless of where you end up or when you run out of fuel.

Frequently, strategic failure may be traced to one of these factors, whether alone or in combination with others. Yet staggeringly often the truth is starker still. Most investors simply never do any proper planning or analysis in the first place. Given the many difficulties that may arise during the process, and the various sensitivities that might need to be accommodated, then it would be tempting to assume that this is because the process has been considered, but then discarded into the 'too dif-ficult' box. Yet this is rarely the case. What is much more common is that the need for strategic vision has simply never occurred to any senior employee within the organisation.

The word 'vision' prompts a couple of interesting points that need to be properly understood before we can travel any further on our journey of discovery. First, vision is not the same thing as strategy. The world is full of chief executives who can talk convincingly and passionately about their organisation's 'vision'. In the event, 'vision' usually turns out to be an emotive and frequently idealised view of the world as one would like it to be. Yet ideals, splendid though they may be in other fields, are dangerous things when it comes to strategy, whether military, corporate or investment. They are noble goals which can be set as outward symbols of the corresponding nobility of thoughts and intentions, yet they are rarely practical ones.

Often they are completely unattainable: sometimes because they involve unrealistic expectations of human behaviour – expecting it to be devoid of greed, fear or self-interest; sometimes because they require levels of technology that do not exist at present; sometimes because they ignore regulatory or other constraints to which the organisation (and others) are subject; and sometimes because they assume a readiness to incur a cost, whether financial or otherwise, that may prove unacceptable.

Strategy is different. Strategy is about what might be achieved in the real world with the resources actually at one's disposal, not what might be achieved in a notional world with the resources one would like to possess, but do not. Strategy is about reality, and translating an actual today into a manageable tomorrow. Vision is about aspiration, and some sort of utopian future.

Second (and this should be apparent from what has just been said), vision has the potential to be a powerfully disruptive element in the strategic process. For the process to achieve a successful outcome requires the rigorous application of reason in analysing the relevant facts and issues. This must by definition be dispassionate, since emotion is the enemy of logic. Yet vision cares little for reason, and can itself be an overwhelming emotional force. It is vision which creates the intellectual no-go areas that effectively doom many strategic reviews to failure from the outset. This is one of several reasons why, as will be explained in Chapter 3, the process is best run by a third party facilitator. An outsider will recognise vision for what it is, and try to keep it locked firmly outside the room while the debate takes place. Yet this itself raises grave difficulties, which we shall explore shortly.

The other problem about vision is that what it represents are essentially the shared values of the members of the organisation. This in turn assumes that the stated vision is the outcome of some sort of *Gestalt*, a collection of human minds that have come together to function as one, rather like a supercomputer. Yet, of course, this is not the case. It really represents what has been called the *koinos kosmos* (shared world).

As individuals, we all have our own personal view of the world, and it seems clear that we all, at least to some extent, alter our perception of reality in an attempt to bring it closer to our beliefs. This is the *idios kosmos* (private world).[7] When the individual becomes part of a group, however, the *koinos kosmos* is adopted instead, which has been described as a diplomatic fiction, or the lowest common denominator of what the group members believe. It is this, incidentally, that probably leads to 'groupthink' – the tendency of any group to think collectively and not to question any conclusion that has been reached, no matter how suspect it might be when viewed by an outsider.

So, frequently, the 'vision' will be fuzzy around the edges, as it is extremely unlikely that every member of the group will share exactly the same values to exactly the same degree. It is possible that this might even be some sort of mental defence mechanism whereby individuals adopt the views of the group as closely as they are able to avoid the stress of conflicting belief systems. At worst, the 'vision' may be nothing more than the strongly expressed views of a forceful chief executive officer (CEO), with everyone else feeling that they have to tag along.

It is unfortunate that some believe that 'vision' should play an important part in strategic planning.[8] Unless vision is being used here in the sense of desired realistic objectives, rather than idealised notional outcomes, then this statement is not only false but also dangerously misleading. Even in public sector areas such as education and health care, reliance on 'vision' will produce a groupthink which states 'This is what we must have; now, how can we find the money?' rather than 'This is how much money we can afford; how can we use it most effectively?'. Again, strategy is about reason, whereas vision is about emotion. This is such a fundamental point that it bears repeating. Vision is about constructing castles in the air. It would be disastrous if this were allowed to serve as the starting point for a strategy of how actually to go and live in them.

---

7. These terms come originally from Heraclitus, but will be familiar to those who have read, or read about, the fiction of Philip K. Dick.
8. See, for example, the Wikipedia 'strategic planning' entry.

2
Emotional Issues and Their Effects

We have described strategy as an intellectual pursuit which produces as its output the optimal approach which is most likely to achieve the desired objectives given all the relevant considerations. This is true in theory, but extremely difficult to accomplish in practice. Because, as has already been noted, at the heart of all business processes, and nowhere more so than in strategic analysis, lurks a potentially fatal paradox. To arrive at the sort of result described above requires that the exercise is carried out totally dispassionately, using reason ruthlessly to pare away all irrelevant issues until the bare bones of the basic logic problem can be discerned and agreed. Yet human beings, or most of them, do not work in this way and are in fact incapable of doing so. Humans are animals, not machines, and react to situations not only with logic, but also with emotion. Psychologists have long recognised that, for many people, the pull of emotion is sufficiently strong as to completely overwhelm their logical functions, particularly when dealing with situations in which they are personally involved.

More recently, psychologists have also started to explore situations in which people *believe* they are acting rationally, but are in fact being manipulated by their emotions without realising it. Any such effect is known as a cognitive bias, and many specific individual ones have been identified. For example, the endowment effect causes us to value something more highly if we already own it than if we do not, and thus can cause us to refrain from selling an asset when disposing of it would in fact be the rational thing to do.

In part this is because the power of emotion is sufficiently strong even to distort our perception. The importance of perception was well recognised by the ancient Greeks 3,000 years ago, though this has not prevented writers on traditional finance theory from completely ignoring it during the last several decades. Plato, for example, gives the well-known example of a group of people who are held prisoner all their lives facing the wall of a cave which is lit by firelight. They will believe, since they know no different, that the shadows which flit across the wall represent reality, since this is what they perceive. It is only if the prisoners are rescued and led out of the cave that they will begin to see reality for what it is.

Though this is a powerful allegory, which Plato uses somewhat arrogantly to exemplify the difference between a philosopher (one who sees reality clearly) and a lesser mortal (who does not), it is in fact not an accurate one, or at least not a complete one. For even a prisoner who is led out of the cave will not see reality as it is, but rather as he perceives it to be. He will see what he believes to be reality on the basis of what is being transmitted to him by his senses and being translated by his brain.

There are two possible things that can go wrong here. First, people's sensory responses may well be different. If one of the prisoners is deaf, or colour-blind, then their sensory experience of life outside the cave will be different from someone else's. Second, we have already seen that the power of emotion, in the form of cognitive biases, can interfere with the translation process, so that what we perceive, which ultimately forms part of our mental process, is not necessarily reality as it is, but reality as we would like it to be. Indeed, some writers, such as Henri Bergson and Aldous Huxley, argued that this was a necessary mechanism for filtering out a reality that might be too rich, or too upsetting for people to deal with. Huxley went further, believing that what appeared to be madness could simply be what happened when this sanitising mechanism failed and people glimpsed reality as it truly was.[1] This idea that 'madness' might actually be a sane reaction to an insane world, first put forward by Huxley in the 1950s, would later be developed by Michel Foucault and R. D. Laing.

Awareness of these issues is essential to a proper understanding of the problems that lie in wait for those embarking on the investment strategy process. We must recognise that our own emotions, and fear most of all, can and will distort our thinking. We cling to what we know, and fear what we do not. We crave that with which we are familiar, and fear change (a subject on which Bergson lectured extensively). We value certainty, and fear uncertainty. Most investors are, for example, prepared to pay a premium for liquidity (perceived certainty), in the shape of accepting a lower return, perhaps even a negative return, and resile unthinkingly from illiquidity (perceived uncertainty), even where it might offer the expectation of a much higher return.

This last element, a disproportionate fear of uncertainty, has a fundamental influence on the strategic process, since it can even influence what

---

1. See Aldous Huxley, *The Doors of Perception*, London, Penguin, 1965.

form it should take. This influence is subtle, yet strong. All that a state of uncertainty implies is that you do not know what will occur. Yet people seem to equate uncertainty with a state of not being in control. This is, of course, a fallacy. Just because you do not know in advance what is going to happen does not mean that you are unable to influence possible outcomes, or to react to change as it occurs. Yet this almost pathological fear of uncertainty creates a cognitive distortion which runs through the entire world of finance and investment.

It is, for example, the driving motive behind so-called 'modern' portfolio theory (this was first advanced in the early 1950s). This posits that risk and uncertainty of outcome are the same thing, and that all the material risk of an investment can be expressed by the volatility of its past periodic returns. In this way, uncertainty itself can be calculated mathematically and is thus tamed in some way. The bogeyman is still hideous and terrifying, but has at least been shackled and caged.

Of course, this is itself a fallacy. You have not measured uncertainty at all. All you have measured is the statistical probability of certain outcomes occurring, based on the entirely irrational assumptions that the future will be a perfect mirror of the past, and that normal distribution will always apply (despite clear evidence that it does not).[2] This also ignores a particular example of what is known as the 'gambler's fallacy' which was pointed out by the great Austrian economist, Ludwig von Mises:[3] just because you know the probability of an event occurring does not mean that the actual outcome will accord with your expectations, particularly within a relatively short period of time, or small number of trials.

Within the investment strategy process, this disproportionate fear of uncertainty manifests itself in a determination to remain firmly rooted in the (perceived) reality of the here and now, and to eschew forays into the quicksand of possible future events. We seek the illusion of control by assuming that whatever applies today is certain and enduring. We avoid, because we fear, the unpleasant suspicion that times will change, and that we will need to change with them. A perfect example of this may be seen in the way in which defined benefit (final salary) pension schemes resolutely ignored for so long the obvious need to increase their longevity assumptions.

The danger is that this sort of thinking may be allowed to close off a whole range of analysis, effectively creating intellectual no-go areas.

---

2. See, for example, Niall Ferguson, *The Ascent of Money*, London, Penguin, 2009, p. 166.

3. Ludwig von Mises, *Human Action*, Ludwig von Mises Institute, Kindle edition, 2009.

Scenario analysis should form an important part of any strategic planning exercise, and to forgo it is akin to asking somebody to understand Judaism and Christianity by reading only the Old Testament.

Scenario analysis has its origins, like so much of strategic theory and practice, in the corridors of military staff colleges. It is a traditional way in which military planners try to deal with conditions of uncertainty. If you do not know which outcomes will actually occur, but can identify a number that you believe may at least be possible candidates, then why not consider them hypothetically in turn? You can then go a stage further and assume that some of them may occur in combination with each other. In this way, a whole suite of possible states of the world, or scenarios, can be built up and planned for.

By the way, the first of these exercises was widely used in classical economics by the likes of Alfred Marshall, under the lofty description *ceteris paribus*. Strictly speaking, this Latin term means 'with all other things being equal (or the same)'. In practice, this means holding all variables except one fixed, and then moving the remaining one around to see what happens. Though mathematically unsatisfactory (since any number of the variables may actually influence any number of the others), this can be a useful analytical exercise.

So it was that the military planners of all the major powers around the world used to prepare, and review annually, plans for a state of war with one, or some combination of, the remaining great powers. Until shortly before the First World War, for example, Britain was planning for possible war with France.

This does not mean that Britain thought war with France highly probable – though there were occasions, such as the Fashoda incident, when it seemed so to the public at large – still less that Britain *intended* war with France. It simply means that Britain thought the possibility of war with France a sufficiently likely event, with a sufficiently important impact should it occur, to plan for it. In practice, largely for emotional reasons, this distinction is not well understood. All too often, admitting that something might happen, by planning for it, is seen as tantamount to accepting that it *will* happen, or even that certain people within the organisation might actually *want* it to happen, perhaps because they can then be proved right in their vision of the future.

Where potentially unpleasant human outcomes are involved, feelings on this point can run high. The suspicious will argue: 'Why plan for something unless you think it is going to happen?' This can be a particularly delicate area in corporate, as opposed to investment, strategy. Modelling a scenario that could result in some reduction in staffing is often seen as unacceptable, for both emotional and practical reasons; should the staff find out, it might not sound over-reassuring for management to say they were simply considering their options.

All of which is unfortunate, since the great attraction of scenario analysis is obvious. By defining the limits within which you are going to consider certain aspects of uncertainty, you can increase your preparedness to face possible outcomes. Whether the event will occur remains doubtful, but if it does occur then its consequences are less likely to take you by surprise. In one of the supreme coincidences of history, for example, the German army were war-gaming an allied invasion of Normandy at the precise moment when the Allies did in fact invade. Furthermore, they were war-gaming what was considered to be a most unlikely scenario created by a maverick general, which in fact mirrored exactly what the Allies had actually chosen to do. Rather than rejoining their headquarters, some staff officers were ordered to remain and play the game to its conclusion, substituting real-life troop dispositions where these could be identified in reports from the field, and feeding back suggested actions.

The greatest attraction of scenario analysis seems, however, also to be its greatest weakness, at least as far as human psychology is concerned. To model a scenario, you have to admit to yourself tacitly that it might actually happen, no matter how remote the possibility. Since the human mind finds, in most cases, uncertainty to be disturbing and unsettling, there is a disinclination to make this tacit admission in the first place. This leads in turn to a strong tendency to consider only what prevails at present (or, at least, that which is *believed* to prevail at present) and to disregard other possible states of affairs. Thus, for most investors, scenario planning forms no part of the strategic process.

What is both surprising and disappointing, however, is that the desire to avoid stressful areas of discussion drives this to extreme lengths. Not only are participants disinclined to consider structural shifts in the surrounding world environment, but also choose to ignore unpleasant truths about their own individual circumstances as an organisation. British pension funds, for example, frequently ignored in their deliberations that they were less than fully funded, presumably trusting, like Charles Dickens' Mr Micawber, that 'something will turn up'. Fortunately for them, it did: the ability simply to wave a white flag and close down their scheme, rather than to plan to make good the deficit – a great victory for these investors, who were able in this way to escape completely having to take responsibility for the consequences of their own actions (or, more accurately, complete lack of action). We shall see in Chapter 4 that we label these sorts of fatalists, who do not believe they can or should take responsibility for events, 'Pierre investors'.

Where scenario planning does exist within an investment organisation, the difference is palpable. Those investors who *do* believe that we can shape events around us ('Maria investors' – see Chapter 4) are currently considering how to preserve the real value of investors' capital in the face of hostile government action, or in periods of high inflation, or even in the aftermath of a collapse of confidence in paper currency. Pierre investors, on the other hand, are simply sitting back and allowing events to flow past them in the time stream, carrying them where they will. Should any of these events occur, then Maria investors will already have considered their consequences, and the required responses. In some cases they will already have taken pre-emptive action.

So, scenario planning should take place within the investment strategy process, but it very rarely does. Instead, a fairly limited set of possible future circumstances tend to be considered, whether with regard to the organisation itself, or to the wider environment generally.

As we can see, then, it is very difficult to stop emotion from leaking into the process. Indeed, it is generally accepted that not only are most people simply unable to divorce their emotions from the decision-making process, but they also see no reason why they should. On the contrary, they are likely to become quite angry with people who do have this ability, who are in turn likely to become quite angry at what they see as cheating, since *they* believe that emotion can and should be reserved for private purposes such as romantic and family relationships, and has no valid role in the workplace.

Emotion can cloud thinking in a number of different ways. It can induce people to choose or reject different objectives, particularly if it becomes clear that some of them can only be achieved at the risk of causing distress to others. It can bring apparently irrelevant factors into play, thus obfuscating the real issues and obstructing constructive discussion. It can make it difficult for participants to challenge the *koinos kosmos*, the accepted norms and attitudes of the group. In particular, it can lead to unwelcome truths about the organisation being filtered out, thus exposing planning to the risk of starting its journey from the wrong point on the map.

Thus a working knowledge of psychology can be an immense help for whoever is selected to run the process. It may not be possible for emotive influences to be stripped out, but at least if the facilitator can recognise them for what they are when they arise, and be able to empathise with the individuals involved, there is a chance that their disruptive effect may at least be in some way reduced or deflected.

Scenario planning is (or should be) an important part of investment strategy. In considering threats and opportunities in the surrounding environment it is important to note not only those that actually exist at present, but also those that *may* exist in the future. Given the current state of uncertainty surrounding economic affairs in general, which is almost certainly far higher than anything we have known before, this process becomes both essential and more challenging.

Once the individual possibilities have been teased out, the challenge is to identify how they may operate upon each other. *Ceteris paribus* is all very well as an intellectual exercise, but real-life events do not prove so co-operative. Some will be mutually exclusive, which is helpful, since clearly they will not have to be modelled together. With others, however, it may prove much more difficult to agree on their interrelationship. How are economic growth and inflation likely to act on each other? How is government likely to react to increased longevity by changing the age of retirement? (This may seem an arcane point to some, but is of vital importance to pension funds.)

Of course, these are subjective judgements, and so any two individuals, let alone any two collectives, are unlikely to agree. Once again, the *koinos kosmos* is likely to come into play. Yet certainly some number of possible scenarios should be delineated and discussed. As Nassim Taleb points out in *Black Swan*,[4] as humans we are likely to ignore possible events which he classifies as low probability but high impact. In other words, if it is felt to be highly unlikely that a particular outcome may arise, yet if it does its effects could be catastrophic, then it would be logical to have a contingency plan in place to deal with the eventuality should it in fact occur. For example, in these times of heavily indebted governments, it may be sensible to imagine a world in which confidence in fiat money has collapsed, no matter how improbable such an outcome may be considered, and it would surely be foolish not even to have considered how such a state of affairs might be dealt with, or how its consequences might be pre-empted, whether in whole or in part. We shall return to this point in Chapter 12.

Sentiment, rather than reason, may affect not just the setting of strategic plans, but also the way in which they are received. Here, a number of powerful emotional drivers may all be at work simultaneously. There is an inbuilt resistance among people to accept decisions to which we have not been party, and with the best will in the world it is impossible to involve more than a relatively small part of an organisation in strategic planning. There is an inbuilt fear of change, and most strategic outcomes will propose at least some changes. There is an inbuilt fear of

4. Nassim Nicholas Taleb, *Black Swan: The Impact of the Highly Improbable*, London: Penguin, 2008.

uncertainty, but a good strategic plan forces us to confront uncertainty rather than to run away from it. There is an inbuilt reluctance to move away from what is known to what is unknown, and any good investment strategy process will almost certainly be proposing a move away from equities and bonds, certainly for long-term investors in the current environment.

A good facilitator can help with this process by preparing the ground in advance, and by the way in which the output documents are phrased. Positive, affirming language will help with emotional acceptance – use of the word 'challenge' instead of 'problem', for example. Yet it is at this point that the CEO, chief investment officer (CIO), or other person charged with overseeing the implementation of the plan, needs to come into their own. She or he needs to take ownership of the plan and communicate it compellingly both downwards to staff and upwards to boards of trustees, non-executive directors and so on. The challenge here is to carry people with you, to induce them to execute the plan because they themselves believe in it, rather than because you are telling them to.

This is a glib, easy thing to say in theory, but a very different proposition in practice. If the strategic process has honestly identified and addressed unwelcome truths, such as a funding deficit, a regulatory block, or a lack of expertise in key areas, then some of the steps recommended may be difficult for some employees to accept. Yet a good communicator will not shrink from this task, and nor should they. With a strategic plan, impetus is everything.

Napoleon Bonaparte said that strategy marches in time and space. Every moment that your chosen strategy is not being executed is a wasted moment. Worse still, every wasted moment makes it less likely that your strategy will prove successful. Within organisations, there is an even deadlier threat: inertia. A plan must be executed, and be seen to be executed, or it risks sinking into the quicksand of inertia, becoming more difficult to rescue with every passing week.

Sadly, investment strategy is often seen as a political football within an organisation, with key individuals obstructing proposals not because they do not believe in them, but simply because the suggestions are seen to be championed by someone else. In these circumstances, surreptitious delaying tactics can mean death by a thousand cuts, or at least by a thousand hiccups in the time stream.

Yet we are getting ahead of ourselves, as we have not yet considered how the process might best be executed, which we shall do in Chapter 3. One hopes, though, we have begun to understand just how complex and challenging the investment strategy process might be. Life is not a game of chess, where all we have to ponder are the available moves; it is a complex interaction of reason and emotion, with emotion being far more powerful in the case of most people. An effective strategic process will recognise how emotion may best be handled, both during the process itself as well as in ways that the output of the process may best be communicated and implemented.

Psychologists now recognise that the old classifications of 'thinking' and 'feeling' advanced by psychologist Carl Jung, while sound, are probably inadequate to explain the full complexity of how people think and behave. For example, is there always necessarily a link between the two? Might much human behaviour be instinctive, such as lifting a glass of water because we want to take a drink, and not really driven by either reason or emotion? However, it does provide a useful starting point, and it would be a great mistake (and one made frequently by the writer in the past) simply to assume that other people will approach any problem in the same way as you do yourself.

Many people are not just unwilling, but apparently also unable to 'think the unthinkable'. Their more dispassionate colleagues might resent, or even despise, this apparent weakness. Similarly, those at the 'feeling' end of the spectrum may be appalled and repelled by what they see as ruthless, cruel and inhuman proposals. Yet any strategic outcome must emanate from a collective organisational view, and this must by definition be some sort of amalgam of differing balances between reason and emotion.

William Shakespeare, as always, understood the human condition. In *Troilus and Cressida* he has the Greeks represent reason and the Trojans emotion. In the first act he shows us the Greek leaders, and in the second act the Trojans, both debating essentially the same point: whether Helen should be returned. Hector (Greek) talks of reason, order and natural law. Troilus (Trojan) speaks of feeling and honour. He brushes logic (a Greek invention) contemptuously aside: 'Nay, if we talk of reason, let's shut our gates and sleep.' This is a reaction that will strike a chord with many who have been frustrated by their colleagues' refusal to think objectively and dispassionately about a particular issue.

Many strategists may feel emotion to be the enemy of the process. Yet we are human, and there are times when emotion can carry us to heights which reason cannot scale. In the summer of 1940, the 'thinkers' such as Lord Halifax (Greek?), pointed out, quite reasonably, that Britain was now all but defenceless, her army having left all its equipment behind at Dunkirk, and in imminent danger of running out of both food and money, and suggested making an approach through Mussolini for a negotiated peace with Hitler. It was the 'feeler', Churchill (Trojan?), the man frequently moved to tears, to the embarrassment of his colleagues, who indignantly rejected any such idea. Similarly, any logical analysis of the American space programme in the early 1960s would probably have concluded that the current state of technology, particularly with regard to computers, rendered the objective (putting a man on the moon) unattainable at that time, and recommended putting everything on hold.

In fact, the situation is more complex and less binary than it has been presented above. The over-simplification is deliberate, since it is essential to get the point across and this is best done as baldly as possible.

Yet, as we have seen, psychologists have long recognised that Jung's delineation of thinking and feeling, while an innovative and insightful step, does not fully explain the ways in which reason and emotion interact in decision-making. A more mainstream approach today looks at no fewer than five factors that might be at play, all interacting with each other: openness, conscientiousness, extraversion, agreeableness and neuroticism. Thus, if plotted graphically, everyone's personality type will appear somewhere on a five-pointed star.

Openness does not mean openness in the sense of being quick to recount and explain one's actions, nor even of being approachable (though both of these qualities will tend to be present), but rather openness to new experiences. These new experiences will include emotional states, and acts of imagination. People who score highly on openness are likely to be creative and imaginative. They are likely to have the ability to present ideas as images, rather than dry textual descriptions. They are likely to juggle many different ideas at the same time, and to make seemingly random mental connections between them. Perhaps, in consequence, they will frequently hold unusual, even seemingly eccentric views.

Conscientiousness brings a need for order and an attention to detail. A neat desktop, always arranged in exactly the same way, is a tell-tale sign here, as is a tendency to take detailed, methodical notes. This personality trait will induce a desire for planning and a mistrust of either improvisation or conceptual speculation. Those who score highly on conscientiousness are likely to fear uncertainty much more than those who are towards the openness point of the star, and thus to over-value certainty in consequence.

Extraversion, and its opposite twin, introversion, are based around the need for, and level of comfort with, human interaction, together with the tendency towards either spontaneous (extraversion) or considered (introversion) action. People at the extreme end of the extravert scale will want not only to be part of a group, but the focal point of it, while their introvert shadow self will be standing on the sidelines, or even have gone off to do something on their own. Extraverts make good talkers, whereas introverts make good listeners. Extraverts make good salespeople, while introverts make good analysts, particularly if they also score highly on conscientiousness.

Agreeableness has a wider meaning than in everyday use. It encompasses a desire to make people happy, and to value doing so. A genuine feeling for the greater good of mankind in general, and a subjection of self-interest to the interests of the group. While these may sound like admirable qualities, they do in fact have their negative aspects from an organisational point of view. Those who score highly on agreeableness tend to be very non-confrontational and over-ready to compromise their position. In approaching any issue, their overriding concern is often simply to reach a consensual outcome, almost regardless of what that is. In the investment strategy process, whenever any hitherto clear issue begins to blur around the edges you can be sure that some strongly agreeable personality types are at work.

Neuroticism: those displaying this trait are not, as many seem to believe, delusional. 'Psychotic' would be a more accurate description of such a state since, though it has a more precise psychological term, it usually implies some loss of contact with reality (assuming for a moment that any such thing as 'reality' actually exists). Neuroticism is, rather, the tendency to experience negative thoughts and states of mind. Those who score highly on this trait are more likely to experience depressive or melancholic spells, and these are also more likely to be prolonged. They will have a tendency to see problems as insuperable barriers to progress, rather than challenges to be overcome. They are nature's worriers, the Woody Allens of the world of investment. When they also score highly on conscientiousness and introversion, such characters can prove to be almost impossible to deal with, and are best exiled to run a branch office in the north of Sweden, where they may feel particularly at home during the winter months.

Readers may wish to pause at this stage and perform some honest five-factor analysis on themselves. It can be a revealing exercise. Don't worry if you end up confused because you seem to share some of the characteristics of each one; that is exactly as it should be. You may find, however, that, say, two out of the five will tend to be more dominant. Now perform the same exercise on those with whom you live or work, but do bear in mind that in order to perform this analysis in the first place you are viewing them through the filter of your own perceptions and preconceptions.

For any facilitator charged with conducting an investment strategy process, such as that described in the Chapter 3, some preliminary five-factor analysis of the proposed participants is essential. 'Facilitator' is a deliberate choice of word. A facilitator is one who makes it easier for a group of people to achieve their common objective. To do this, it is important to have a feeling of how the group is likely to react to certain ideas, both as a group (*koinos kosmos*) and as individuals (*idios kosmos*), and both of these are likely to be strongly influenced by their personality types and instinctive emotional responses.

Should any measure of success be achieved in gauging the personality factors of oneself and others, and how these may play out both in general and in specific situations, the phrase 'emotional intelligence' may be applied. From a pedantic point of view the expression can be attacked, since 'intelligence' has various precise meanings in academic circles, only some of which (self-awareness, understanding and so on) could be applied in this context. However, on the basis that we have clearly defined what we mean, let us banish the pedants to the glossary of oblivion.

In seeking to define the objectives of any investor, and how these might best be achieved, we need to conduct a strategic process. To give the chosen approach the highest possible chance of success, the process needs to be conducted as well as possible. Should the facilitator have an awareness and understanding of the various emotions in play, and of the personality factors that drive these, then the chances of the process being well conducted rise significantly.

In other words, it is not enough for investment to be intelligent. It must also be emotionally intelligent.

3
Conducting the Process

The strategic process is very much an intellectual journey. For most participants, once they get the idea of what is required, it proves a hugely enjoyable one. Using your mind in a way which is totally different from its normal day to day operational requirements can be a liberating experience, witness the huge popularity of strategy modules at business schools. However, there is also a practical process which allows the intellectual one to take place within it, and it would be as well to be clear from the outset about which matters might make a successful outcome more or less likely.

Who should run it?

The process will not run itself, and the choice of the right person to do so ('the facilitator') can make or break it in terms of likely success.

There will be a natural tendency for the senior professional (let's call him or her the CEO for ease of reference, though in practice such a person is likely to have a different title) to take ownership of the investment strategy and lay out both the timeline of the process and the parameters for discussion. Though this is quite naturally expected, they should probably resist this impulse unless they have some specific strategic expertise, for several reasons.

First, the best strategic discussion requires a certain distancing effect, the ability to rise above everyday events and look down on them, hence the expression 'helicopter view'. By definition, this will be that much more difficult for someone who is intimately involved in those everyday events taking place at the tactical and operational levels than for someone who is not.

Second, and a related point, while intense self-scrutiny is a necessary requirement, so too is a knowledge and appreciation of the wider environment, and someone who has experience of how other investors think and act will have an advantage over someone who only has a deep know-ledge of the organisation itself.

Third, the process requires unflinchingly honest and sincere input from all participants, and this can be very difficult where the person running the process is also the one who is the key to an individual's future career advancement (or otherwise). I well remember one CEO gazing after a departing off-site participant in a rather menacing fashion and saying ominously 'That was very useful – I never knew he felt like that'. As we shall see, if the process is run by an outsider then there are at least some things that can be done to alleviate this problem.

Fourth, the facilitator should ideally be someone who keeps the process on track, and controls the scope and focus of its discussions, but does not seek to influence or contribute to the actual outcome. It is that person's responsibility to see that the process is properly conducted, and not to bring their own opinions to bear on the rival merits of different possibilities. It will prove very difficult for any CEO to fulfil this role.

So, who is the best person to run it? In the case of an investor, such as a pension fund, that relies on a permanent consultant, then the next natural candidate after the CEO may well be seen as that consultant. Again, this option should be resisted, no matter how charmingly and persuasively it is argued, for a number of reasons.

First, human nature being what it is, there will be a natural but regret-table instinct to regard the process itself, and anyone appointed to run it, as a threat. The view will be 'I'm here already to give these people advice on their investments, so why on earth are they looking elsewhere?'. Indeed, the most common reason for the process not occurring at all is that the person who arguably should have initiated strategic discus-sion has not done so, and probably for this reason. Perhaps under pres-sure from lawyers and insurers, there seems to be a natural tendency for investment consultants to refrain from giving positive advice wherever possible, and restrict themselves to supplying information on request.

Second, the consultant will already have taken the investor down a par-ticular path over the years and there will be very powerful reasons, both psychological and political, why that consultant is unlikely to vary any advice has been given in the past.

Third, different consultants will have different strengths and weak-nesses within their own firms, and there will be a natural tendency to push the investor towards those areas in which they have demonstrable high-level expertise and away from those where they do not. To do other-wise would risk losing at least part of their mandate.

Finally, and this point is often overlooked, where a pension fund is concerned, the consultant will usually also be acting also for the spon-sor of the fund (the employer) and so will have a conflict of interest, particularly where the scheme is formally in deficit. The sponsor's interest (to keep the accounting values of assets and liabilities as closely synchronised as possible) is clearly not the same as that of the fund itself (to have sufficient money in the future to be able to pay the pension liabilities as they fall due).

Of course, it would be a nonsense to finalise investment strategy without regard to the circumstances and attitude of the sponsor, but it is for the fund's trustees to set the strategy, not the sponsor, and they should not shirk that duty. They should first set out what they feel the optimum strategy should be, and then discuss with the sponsor how they might react to it. As we shall see, this is a circular process, or risks becoming so. If, for example, the fund has made certain assumptions about contributions being forthcoming from the sponsor and then learns that it is mistaken, this will increase the required target rate of return, leading to a new strategy and fresh discussions.[1]

It will, though, be very difficult to set the optimum strategy in the first place if the process is being run by a third party who is being paid by the sponsor. It is a failure to recognise this issue that is responsible for the fact that, in so far as it exists at all, most pension fund 'strategy', certainly in the UK, is designed for the accounting convenience of the sponsor, not the future funding needs of the plan.

The remaining candidates are probably just two: either a chairman or other non-executive, or an outsider such as an independent consultant. The first can work very well, since such an individual will typically have experience not just of the organisation, but also of others who may be confronting similar issues and examining similar options. They may also themselves have a background in investment management. However, two requirements should be fulfilled for such an appointment to be contemplated. First, the individual should have some experience of having run a strategic process in the past. As we shall see in the next section, this is quite a specialist skill. Second, given what we have already said about the role of CEOs, they must be genuinely independent in the sense of having an arm's-length relationship with the CEO. They must also be someone in whom the other participants can have absolute trust not to disclose anything they are told in confidence.

Where these two conditions are satisfied, such an individual will usually be an ideal choice as facilitator. Where they are not, then the appointment of an independent third party should be strongly considered.

---

1. The Pensions Regulator exists to resolve, in the case of a UK scheme in deficit, any possible logjam in this process. However, the government has not seen fit to extend this protection to public sector occupational schemes, whose liabilities the government itself guarantees. Different systems and bodies exist in other countries.

The role of facilitator

The process will stand or fall on the performance of the facilitator, and this person's role begins well before the first meeting is held.

The sorts of issues to be discussed are set out later in the book. These should be circulated to all participants for advance consideration, and if at all possible the facilitator should hold a private session with each individual, canvassing their views on a confidential basis. In this way, the facilitator can say during a meeting 'another point which came up in my discussions was…' without the originator of the comment being identified.

Ideally, the strategic process, having such a huge potential impact on performance, would take up most of the board's time, and discussions could thus be spread over several days. In reality, the situation is different, however, largely because the vital importance of strategy is widely misunderstood. It is possible, therefore, that as little as a single day may be set aside. In this case, the facilitator must try to anticipate all issues that might arise and, as far as possible, have material prepared on these in advance.

Once discussions begin, it is the task of the facilitator to keep them on track. This is not as easy as it sounds. Most people have a tendency to stray from one issue to another, and this will not do. The facilitator must insist that the group finishes with one issue (or at least comes to some tentative conclusions) before moving on to the next. Where issues relate to others that have already be discussed, it is the facilitator's job to ask the meeting to check back and see if it is satisfied that the decisions reached are consistent with the earlier outcomes.

Above all, the facilitator must see to it that all reactions to input are non-judgemental. This is particularly important in strongly hierarchical organisations, where one senior figure may easily dominate the meeting if allowed to do so. Frequently, the more stupid a question might seem, and the more hesitantly it is asked, the more valid it is, since it will frequently challenge some long-accepted assumption. It is the task of the meeting above all to draw out exactly such questions; remember our friend 'Why?'.

It will be a matter of personal style how the facilitator decides to do this. In some cultures it will be necessary to be deferential, and thus tactful, to senior figures. In others, a more informal approach may be tried. I experimented for a time with a football referee's whistle, and red and yellow cards. Whatever the method, the facilitator must ensure that the meeting stays on track, that everyone is drawn into the discussion, and that input is received in a non-judgemental fashion.

After the verbal discussions are complete, it will generally fall to the facilitator to put the agreed strategy in writing. Here, less is more. It is far better to state baldly the fundamental conclusions reached rather than to try to flesh out the minutiae. The more content there is, the more likely it is that someone who is ill-disposed to the conclusions can take issue with it. The less detail provided, the easier it is to mould tactics to fit the strategy. Remember that this is largely about *what* will be done, and *why*. The *how* and *when* are really tactical considerations and can be deferred for future discussion or, best of all, delegated whenever possible for immediate attention by others who are empowered to make decisions.

There are, in fact, a few important exceptions to this principle, which will become clear later, but which will be ignored for our present purposes.

Who should participate?

It is most important that the person/people who is/are going to take responsibility for actually executing whatever strategy is decided upon should take part in the process. This will normally mean the person with overall authority over the investment process, and this is important, since in many cases that person is surprisingly excluded from the asset allocation decision process, with these being taken by trustees or non-executive board members. This is deeply illogical. As we have seen, it is the strategic decisions that will drive almost all of the organisation's outperformance, and so not only should a great deal of time be devoted to these, but so also should the expertise of any available senior level investment professionals. In addition, a chief investment officer (CIO) is (or should be) unwilling to take responsibility for the performance of a portfolio which they have had no part in structuring.

A useful addition to the process can be someone who has recently retired from a senior investment role elsewhere. Not only will such a person bring great breadth of knowledge and experience, but their status as an 'outsider' can be of great assistance in challenging the accepted dogma of conventional wisdom that often takes root within an organisation. The facilitator should be alert to this possibility, and perhaps even prime the individual in advance as to certain issues they might consider raising.

Incidentally, if all this sounds over-political, or as if it is dwelling too much on the human aspects of the discussion, then it is possible that you have never participated in a process such as this. If you have, then you have been almost unbelievably fortunate if it has run smoothly and come to a good conclusion. In practice, the process is frequently frustrated by human issues, most usually by one strong character in a senior position stubbornly refusing to accept that there is anything wrong with the way things are already being done (and probably have always been done). Such an individual can quickly divert discussion from the strategic level altogether, whether intentionally or not, into things such as how manager selection gets carried out.

It is therefore essential that the facilitator should be alert to any emotional or other behavioural factors, and try to plan in advance ways to forestall them.

Where should it happen?

It is strongly recommended that the group discussion parts of the process be carried out off-site, at a hotel or conference centre, for example. This will frequently be resisted, on the grounds of cost or convenience. Since many senior executives are extremely bad delegators, you may also get objections such as 'I can't afford to take a whole day out of the office'.

A good facilitator will insist, quietly but firmly, that it is essential to move the discussion off-site. First, there is the psychological advantage of physically distancing yourself from tactical and operational matters. Second, despite how many promises are made to the contrary in advance, people *will* be called out of the meeting to take a telephone call, or will disappear for a coffee break and not come back.

It should be made clear that this is the most important discussion it is possible for the organisation to have. A note should placed in the diary well ahead of time, communicating the clear message that the date will not be changed under any circumstances. Naturally, all this will require the support of those at the top of the organisation, so it is vital that they at least recognise the fundamental importance of what is involved.

On arrival at the venue, all mobile phones and other electronic devices should be switched off and handed over for the day. Again, the facilitator should insist on this.

How should the discussion be organised?

Since there is usually a very poor understanding of what strategy actually is, it is often a good idea to begin with a brief explanation, and this is something which can best be done by the facilitator. Of course, if all attendees are given this book to read in advance, then this part of the proceedings can be kept as short as possible!

It is frequently helpful to then have a brief brain-storming session on some totally unrelated topic, such as the possible uses to which an empty bucket might be put. This provides an opportunity to explain the rules of the game about judgemental comment, helps to break the ice (everyone can be forced to contribute by going round the table in turn, if desired), and helps to free minds up to think in a different way.

It is then the facilitator's task to 'walk' the group steadily through the process, considering in turn the various issues that will be identified in the following chapters. It is important that the facilitator controls the discussion without actually contributing to it, which is a very delicate balance to maintain. Generally, the facilitator should intervene only for the purposes of clarification (if unsure of someone's precise meaning, or is concerned that two separate issues are becoming confused, for example), keeping the discussion on track ('Hang on, let's deal with one issue at a time, please'), or moving on to the next subject. They also have the responsibility of seeing that everyone contributes, and that one or two individuals don't hog the discussion.

How frequently should the process be repeated?

The most important occasion on which the strategic process is run is the first one, since, if well conducted, this will have set the organisation broadly on the right path, so that discussion can then tend safely towards the specifics of tactical and operational matters. Indeed, if the process takes places only once, the organisation will already be enjoying a clear competitive advantage, since in the case of the overwhelming majority of investors around the world the process *never* takes place at all.

How often it should be repeated is a matter for the individual organisation, and will depend partly on the amount of time that can be spared (and in practice this is very little, and granted only grudgingly), and partly on where the investor stands on the long-term/short-term continuum. This latter point will not mean very much at the moment, but will become clearer in due course.

There may in fact be a tendency to repeat the process too often. This can be very dangerous, because there will be a temptation to tinker with earlier decisions, and this militates against agreeing a consistent long-term approach and sticking to it. Indeed, some believe that there may be a negative correlation between the returns of a portfolio and the frequency with which its constituents are changed. The writer heard this view expressed once at an investment conference in America as 'the more often you look at your portfolio, the worse you are likely to do'.

Ideally, the process will result not just in an agreed asset mix, but also in an agreement to rebalance the portfolio, whether once a year, once every six months, or once every quarter. Since rebalancing should be an automatic process, this can and should be delegated, and should require no further sign-off by the board or investment committee.

The best practice is probably for the participants to set aside between half a day and one whole day a year (which for many boards will constitute one of their four quarterly meetings) specifically to consider whether any changes have occurred that might merit a change in the agreed strategy. These could be specific to the organisation, or refer to its immediate environment (such as regulatory changes that apply to particular classes of investor), or have occurred within the world at large, particularly if they are specific to one of the asset types selected for investment (or may make one previously rejected more attractive).

Even here, though, it is important to keep one's eyes fixed firmly on the horizon. All too often someone will venture a view such as 'I don't think this is a good time to be investing in equities' – a statement that may be suspect for many reasons. First, if one is investing with a time frame of many years in mind, then short-term fluctuations are irrelevant and, as will be explained later, might actually be beneficial. Second, if one has agreed automatic rebalancing, then such fluctuations are smoothed away and used to advantage. Third, the maker of the statement may often be worried about a falling market rather than a rising one, and becoming a victim of the emotional pressures that drive many investors to sell low and buy high.

Once one is happy that a sensible long-term approach has been agreed, there should be great reluctance to start changing allocation classes and levels, compared to simply rebalancing. The times when a genuine structural change occurs that will render an asset type significantly less attractive in the long term are rare and, in any event, can usually only be spotted in retrospect rather than in advance. Always remember Michael Porter's words: 'strategy must have continuity. It can't be constantly reinvented'.[2]

What should the output be?

The paper produced by the process should state the conclusions the participants have agreed, the objectives that have been identified, and the method chosen to attempt to achieve them. It should also make clear which specific risks have been identified, and to what extent the chosen strategy seeks to lessen their possible impact.

The paper has three main purposes, though these may differ from one organisation to another. First, it focuses the participants' minds on what has been discussed and agreed, giving them a last chance to correct any mistakes. However, it should be made clear that this is not

---

2. Keith M. Hammond, 'Michael Porter's Big Ideas', available at www.fastcompany. com.

an opportunity for revisiting or reopening the conversation, merely for checking that the summary is indeed an accurate record of what has been discussed and agreed.

Second, it will serve as the input for the tactical part of the programme. This will probably not be relevant to all the participants in the strategic programme, not least because some of them may have been present in a non-executive capacity, but will usually involve at least some of those who are responsible operationally for giving effect to it, together with some new additions, who may be specialists with expertise either in particular functions (settlement, regulations, manager selection and so on) or specific investment areas.

This new team will be tasked with turning the strategic plan into a practical investment programme. While this will involve considerations that are essentially tactical rather than strategic, it may none the less be convenient to see it as an extension of the strategic process, at least in so far as it will enable a feedback loop to operate. If the strategic process has reached certain conclusions on the assumption that certain things will be possible, or can be done in a certain way, and the tactical analysis then shows that in fact such an assumption is flawed, this should be referred back to the strategy team to see if they would like to change their minds based on what is actually possible rather than what they believed to be desirable.

Examples of this often occur when detailed regulatory advice becomes available, or it becomes apparent that management, dealing or other charges are going to be much higher than was originally anticipated. There may also be items that have simply not been considered, such as the length of time taken to put capital to work in certain asset types (notably private equity, infrastructure and real estate), and what should be done with this money in the meantime.

Third, the strategy paper may often have to be disclosed to third parties, or even to the public at large. In many jurisdictions, for example, pension funds have to make available a Statement of Investment Principles, which is (or, more accurately, should be) the output of an investment strategy process. In this case it may be felt desirable that the principles should be stated as generally as possible, but at the very least allocation levels between asset types should be given, together with the reasoning behind them having been set at these levels.

What happens next?

I hope that, by your having read even this far, it will be apparent that it is simply not possible to write a prescriptive guide to investment strategy, certainly not in the same way that one could, for example, write a workshop manual on how to strip the engine on a particular model of car. One can certainly lay down normative statements about what *should* happen, but even this is difficult in more than the most general terms, since organisations are structured differently, have different methods of governance and decision-making, and, of course, have different degrees of freedom of action. It would not be reasonable, for example, to expect a heavily regulated public sector body to operate internally in the same way as a private client's wealth manager, nor the sovereign wealth fund of a largely authoritarian government to work in the same way as a small family office in New York or London.

All too often, of course, the strategic process is never implemented in the first place, so one should be grateful for any sort of strategic output at all. Problems can still arise, however, either where the output is not really strategic in the first place, or when it is regarded as an end in itself and is never implemented but quietly forgotten about.

Where the first of these problems arises, it is usually because the process has not been conducted properly, with the strategic level being completely skipped and discussion moving straight to things such as optimum levels of asset allocation, and the number of managers. Obviously, in the absence of strategic parameters, any such discussion is essentially sterile, but the fact that it can and does happen, being passed off routinely as 'strategy', demonstrates all too clearly just how little understanding of the true nature of strategy actually exists within the industry.

Further planning exercises and behavioural considerations

Ideally, once the strategic plan has been prepared, the further planning referred to above can begin. This will investigate, in so far as investigation is needed, exactly how the asset allocation agreed upon can best be implemented. This will involve discussions of exactly *how* this coverage can best be obtained in each case, and the sorts of issues that will be considered are discussed in subsequent chapters.

Very few investors will have specialist knowledge about different asset types available in-house, apart from possibly fixed income and quoted equities, and even then perhaps only partially; emerging markets, for example, may represent a particular knowledge gap. This process will therefore necessarily involve seeking such knowledge from outside, and this is where consultants can prove particularly useful, especially those who specialise in a particular asset class.

Be aware, though, that considerable filtering may have gone into whatever you are told. Generalist consultants have traditionally discouraged forays into so-called 'alternative' assets (anything other than bonds or equities) because they lacked the specialist expertise to cover them credibly (though this is now changing). Real estate consultants will typically focus on their own domestic market, plus perhaps (if asked) one or two others, because that is where they have their own personal contacts and market knowledge. Specialists in other areas are likely to consider only those well-established managers who have registered with them and for whom they have already done some work, thus closing the door to what might actually be very exciting emerging managers. Finally, no consultant is ever likely to recommend what is called passive investing (which will be explained and explored later in the book), since such an approach renders consultants unnecessary, except to a very limited degree.

So, be aware of what you are getting. Value it for the specific data-points it offers, but remember that the recommendations (if you are lucky enough to get any – most investment consultants avoid giving specific advice) are loaded with a certain amount of subjective framing (see below) and assumptions. It is therefore recommended that you supplement this by going out and speaking to people in the industry for yourself. In some extreme cases you may even discover that a whole avenue of approach has simply been omitted, perhaps because there is as yet insufficient data available on it, or because someone within the consultancy instinctively mistrusts it. Beware too of situations where either the input or the output values of data analysis have simply been made up (though the consultant will usually say 'assumed').

In order to understand properly what goes on here, it may be worth looking in passing at two particular cognitive biases that crop up frequently during the investment strategy process: framing and confirmation bias. Framing is the tendency to limit the discussion of a particular subject by considering only certain aspects of it, or certain possible causes and effects. Like all cognitive biases, it is (subconsciously and thus unintentionally) self-serving. The framing selected is based on the individual's existing beliefs. This in turn flows across into the *koinos kosmos*, manifesting itself as part of groupthink, particularly where the team is tight-knit and long established and/or where the views are firmly held by a forceful team leader. Rather than imagining this as a window frame, a rather better image might be that of a horse wearing blinkers. There is actually a great deal of the surrounding landscape that the horse never perceives because it is restricted to staring straight ahead; that is, after all, the whole point of putting a horse in blinkers. Framing seems to assume that we, like a skittish horse, might be easily distracted or even disturbed by seeing what is actually out there rather than just what someone thinks is good for us to see.

Confirmation bias is perhaps the biggest curse it is possible to visit on the investment strategy process, since it is both one of the most disruptive and one of the most powerful of the cognitive biases. Briefly, it is the tendency to seek out data that confirms your existing beliefs and ignore or belittle facts that do not. More dangerously still, it includes the tendency not just to fail to give contradictory evidence its due weight, but actually to falsify it.

This happens most often when calculating the 'risk-adjusted' returns of different asset types. Should the output show what some believe to be an inconsistent result ('that's ridiculous, everyone knows that x is riskier than y') they deal with this not by querying the nature of the measure being used, or the type of data, or its means of preparation, but simply by changing either the input or the output figures to produce what they regard as a more seemly result.

We shall deal more fully with this particular problem later in the book, but briefly it is arguably the result of using both the wrong definition of risk and the wrong sort of returns data. Just for good measure (no pun intended) the actual technique employed, the Sharpe ratio, was never intended to be used to compare different asset types against each other, but rather to measure the relative 'risk' (actually volatility) of different assets of the same type (quoted equities) within a single asset class portfolio. It is important to understand this and not be afraid to point it out, since it is a common error you will meet literally on a daily basis within the world of investment.

So, here are all sorts of potential barriers, many of them psychological, to pushing this tactical planning exercise through to a conclusion. However, it is most important that this should be done, lest the strategic process lose its impetus and become bogged down in the quicksands of corporate inertia – an ever-present danger. Always be aware that there will be some within the organisation who see strategy as being unnecessary or, worse still, a threat, and should they have been unsuccessful in stopping the process from being initiated and carried this far, the minutiae of tactical and operational implementation offer wonderful opportunities for seeking further clarification, asking for consultants' reports, checking regulatory points, and generally trying to inflict death by a thousand cuts on the rapidly waning enthusiasm of those remaining few who are still trying to push things forward.

The final problem is that many investment organisation seem to experience frequent changes of leadership, and each new CEO or CIO seems intent on being seen as a breath of fresh air with a 'We're going to do things differently around here from now on' attitude. If an investment strategy process is under way when such a handover occurs, it is almost certain to be shelved. The best that can be hoped for in such circumstances is that you might be able to get it started all over again, but with a whole new set of pre-existing beliefs to handle.

Perhaps all this serves to explain why it is all too easy to get depressed and give up when trying to push the strategic rock uphill against a mixture of prejudice, ignorance and political infighting. It will also help to explain why so very few investors ever even attempt it, much less complete it successfully. For the remainder of the book, however, let us assume that you are lucky enough to be working with one of the very few organisations that recognises the importance of evolving the best possible strategy, is open to new ideas, relatively unencumbered by petty regulation, and is blessed with short lines of communication and speedy decision processes.

So, let us now press ahead and examine what sorts of issues we need to consider when setting out on our strategic journey of exploration.

4
What Sorts of Investor Are We? Different Perspectives on Liquidity and Volatility

It is time to start looking at the different stages of the strategic process, and the issues that arise in each. As we have already seen, working out where you are starting from is at least as important as working out where you want to get to, and the next few chapters will focus on how you go about indentifying exactly what sort of investor you are.

At the heart of this process is the first step that is perhaps the most vital one of all, but one that many investors never consider. This is often because the issue is obscured by regulatory concerns. It can also be because those advising the investor do not appreciate the need to address it. This, in turn, arises because of a couple of fundamental differences in mental outlook which exercise such a powerful influence that we need to identify and describe them at the outset.

Pierre and Maria

The first seems to emanate from something as fundamental as the basic personality type of those who come to the whole business of investment, and can perhaps best be illustrated by two characters from Leo Tolstoy's *War and Peace*: Pierre Bezhukov and Maria Bolkonskaya.

Pierre is a fatalist, or at least that is the way he is presented for most of what is a very long story. He believes that events happen to us and around us, and that we are their prisoners, powerless to influence them, and so there is little point in trying. This is juxtaposed to a corresponding lack of faith in the power of the human will. For example, Pierre finds himself marrying a woman without really knowing why, and going to war when he had originally thought he would do no such thing, and recognising that, short-sighted, soft and disorganised, he is hopelessly unsuited for such an undertaking. When he does finally attempt a conscious act of will it is almost as though he has chosen something he knows in advance is so taxing that he must surely fail. His self-imposed mission to assassinate Napoleon is predictably unsuccessful.

Maria, on the other hand, does not believe in sitting back and waiting for things to happen. She prefers to shape events to her own will, and intervenes decisively when she can – for example to reject a suitor whom all her relatives wish her to marry. Since she is impoverished at this stage in the story (she later becomes wealthy), this is a courageous decision, since she risks having to endure a life of hardship for the sake of not frustrating her own aspirations. *War and Peace* probably has a valid claim to be recognised as the first existentialist novel, with characters attempting to make sense of their own sense of self in the face of apparently overwhelming world events.

Most investors behave as either Pierre or Maria. Pierre investors believe their only responsibility is to put together what seems like a sensible portfolio of assets (for 'sensible' read 'whatever everyone else is doing'), and then sit back and observe the results. For them, investment happens in a vacuum, and the aspirations of the individual investor are irrelevant. Maria investors, on the other hand, believe that all that matters is whether an investor is able to achieve their own personal objectives, and that this outcome can be influenced directly by their own actions. Thus for Pierre investors, analysing what an investor's objectives might be never enters their heads, while for Maria investors it is in a sense all that matters.

Pierre investors would advocate a pension fund investing in exactly the same way if it was 60 per cent funded as if it was 100 per cent funded. Maria investors would at least enquire as to the possibility of making good the funding deficit through investment performance. Pierre investors will set some arbitrary yardstick, such as 'inflation plus 1 per cent' as the investor's performance benchmark. Maria investors will try to calculate what precise target rate of return the investor needs to achieve to meet its objectives.

From this difference of mind-set flows one crucial difference in procedure. For Pierre investors, asset allocation is essentially an input into the strategic process, whereas for Maria investors it is the output. Pierre investors will choose some asset types and allocation levels almost at random. In so far as they are chosen with reference to anything, that 'anything' is likely to be what similar investors are known to be doing. Maria investors will attempt to analyse the amounts and timings of future cash needs, and try to select the mix of assets most likely to be able to provide these as the need arises.

Pierre investors fail to recognise the need for investment strategy, and, even if they did, would fail to spot its only logical starting point: setting the objectives of the investor. Maria investors instinctively grasp both instantly.

One hopes it will be obvious that, for a Pierre investor, the question 'What sort of investor am I?' will be irrelevant, if only because for such an investor *all* strategic questions are irrelevant. Strategy is about making choices between alternative courses of action, and seeking to change things, or at least to influence events, and none of these things form any part of the thinking of a Pierre investor. The next time you sit in a board or investment committee meeting, listen to what is going on around you and make an honest assessment of whether your organisation represents Pierre or Maria. The overwhelming majority are in the former category.

So, these factors can get in the way of an investor ever embarking on the very first stage of the strategic process, which is to answer the question: am I a long-term or a short-term investor? As we shall see, the response to this query is hugely important, since long- and short-term investors should view many things in totally different ways. What is desirable to a long-term investor can be undesirable to a short-term one, and vice versa.

Long- and short-term investors

The question of whether you are a long-term or short-term investor is a crucial one to answer, since totally different principles apply in each case. This makes it all the more remarkable that it is one which, far from addressing, most investors totally fail even to recognise. Equally, however, when they *do* 'get it', it is a truly liberating experience. It is as if they have broken out of their dark prison cell and see for the first time just how wonderful the real, broad landscape can be, compared to the occasional tantalising glimpse of it caught through the window bars.

For the distinction between long- and short-term investing is fundamental, and if you do not understand it then you can never truly understand any important aspect of investment at all, no matter how good you may be at working out bond yields or standard deviations. It is the first building block of the strategic process, and by far the most important, since it is the one on which all the subsequent ones will rest.

Before proceeding further let us be clear about one thing. Most investors will be investing for both the long and short term at the same time. In other words, they may need to think about two separate portfolios rather than a single one. However, the size that each bears relative to the other will vary enormously. Our first tasks, then, are to appreciate the difference between them and to assess how large a portion of our total assets each should represent.

An important clue as to how we might go about these tasks has already been given when we talked about the way in which Maria investors view the world. They will first attempt to analyse the key objectives of any investor, and so should we. We do this by reference to their known and anticipated liabilities as they may arise in the future. There are two separate but related tests we should apply:

1. How far into the future are the liabilities, or some part of them, likely to occur?
2. To what extent are the liabilities, or some part of them, predictable either as to their timing or their amount?

The words 'or some part of them' are highly significant. In the case of many investors, such as family offices, pension funds, life insurance companies, endowments and foundations, their liabilities stretch far into the future and it makes sense to analyse separately those that are anticipated to occur over the next few years (which are likely to be largely predictable in relative terms), and those that will arise further into the future (where uncertainty necessarily increases).

Some investors, such as sovereign wealth funds, may not have any obvious specific liabilities at all. In such cases they should be invited to choose a period over which they wish to have relative certainty of outcome. In the same way, the likes of pension funds should be asked to come to a view on how many years into the future they wish to plan specifically for their liabilities, beyond which they will be happy to adopt a more general approach. Thus, to the dismay of those who believe that finance is simply a sub-set of mathematics, subjectivity imposes itself at the very beginning of the process. No two groups of people are likely to arrive at exactly the same view of an identical set of circumstances, and that is as it should be, since it represents the normal workings of not only reason but also emotion, perception and personality types.

Incidentally, for the avoidance of doubt, the period specified is a *rolling* period with a new quarter being added on to the end of it every time the current quarter expires, so the period chosen need not be a long one: between two and five years should normally suffice.

On the other hand, there are some types of investors, such as banks and non-life insurance companies, whose liabilities can arise at very short notice and in very large amounts. One of the many mistakes that contributed to the banking crisis which began to unfold in 2007 was the illusion that bank runs had in some way been rendered impossible. They hadn't, and some institutions such as Northern Rock paid the price when the wholesale funding on which they had traditionally relied dried up abruptly. In such cases, it almost certainly makes sound sense to assume that *all* one's liabilities are both short-term and unpredictable.

Liquidity

Why should we ask the two questions set out above in particular? Because they determine an investor's need for liquidity, and thus in turn the sorts of assets that are eligible for inclusion in their portfolio. Yet before we can turn to liquidity we need to ask ourselves some important questions which, in practice, amazingly, investors never actually address. Many of them seem very certain that they need and want liquidity but accept this as some sort of religious creed beyond which they feel unable to look. These questions never get asked, yet they are crucial. What is liquidity? Why do we need it? How should we achieve it? Is it a good thing or a bad thing?

Liquidity in this context simply means the ability to generate cash at a moment's notice. If an asset can be exchanged for cash instantly, whatever the circumstances, then it is a liquid asset. If not, then it is, at least to some extent, illiquid. This is the only function of liquidity and the only reason for holding liquid assets within a portfolio. It is the ability to turn assets into cash with no problem or delay. It is a means to an end, not an end in itself. It can never be right to hold liquid assets 'because we need liquidity', but only 'because we may need instant access to cash'.

Thus liquidity can never be a good thing or a bad thing when considered in isolation, but only when viewed in the context of the particular circumstances of an individual investor. In the case of a bank, for example, it absolutely *does* need liquidity, and nowadays regulations force banks to hold a certain proportion of liquid assets, such as government bonds. Yet even banks have many assets on their balance sheets that are not liquid, most obviously loans they have extended to their customers and may not be repayable for some years. Yes, given time, they would probably be able to package these up and sell them off, but 'given time' is an important qualification. To be truly liquid, an asset must be one for which a public market exists, with instant trading and prompt cash settlement.

Yet even this definition does not really fit the bill, because, back in September 2008 in the aftermath of the collapse of Lehman Brothers, the corporate bond market simply curled up and died for a few weeks. Some US pension funds were, for example, trying to sell good quality corporate bonds during this period to honour capital calls from private equity funds, but were unable to do so, a phenomenon that subsequently became known as 'Cash-22', a situation where an investor is rich in asset values, but unable to turn these assets quickly and easily into cash.

So, if the events of 2008 taught us anything, it was that in abnormal market conditions (and arguably it is precisely during abnormal market conditions that one really *needs* liquidity) then the only assets that can guarantee true liquidity are prime government bonds, which have traditionally been reckoned to be those issued by the governments of the US, the UK, Japan and Germany. It remains to be seen to what extent these assets retain such a perceived status in the future.

There are, of course, two other asset types that can be turned quickly and easily into cash: physical gold (which has been described as a currency without a country); and active currency (which is money already). Interestingly, both have been largely ignored by institutional investors, perhaps for reasons of volatility, which we shall discuss separately later in this chapter.

Quoted equities are also, of course, liquid, at least in technical, legal terms. However, disposing of a large equity portfolio in highly nervous market conditions is not an easy task, particularly if one is desperate for instant cash. Here, again, volatility rears its head.

Thus in the case of a short-term investor, one who may have a sudden and/or unpredictable need for cash. it is considerations of liquidity that must dominate and determine the composition of the portfolio. The same is, of course, true of the 'short-term' portfolio of an investor who is treating the liabilities of different time periods in different ways, as outlined above.

The sad and simple truth here is that only prime government bonds can fully satisfy this requirement. Yes, an investor might decide to mix in a judicious sprinkling of corporate bonds, or non-prime government bonds, but this should be done with the express knowledge and acceptance that if one does so, then guaranteed liquidity in abnormal market conditions is being compromised, and given the very grave consequences that might follow should such liquidity be required and be found wanting, it is difficult to advocate any such course. Short-term portfolios should be designed solely with liquidity in mind, and liquidity is most likely to become an issue when markets are in turmoil.

A sad truth, because at the time of writing prime government bond yields offer a negative real return, and thus anybody holding them is guaranteed to lose money after the effects of inflation. While there are particular reasons for this at present, not least the fact that various governments have effectively created a false market in their own bonds through a mix of regulation (such as Basel III and Solvency II) and quantitative easing programmes, it is not a new phenomenon. The myth that holding bonds necessarily gives you a hedge against inflation is just that – a myth. For example, had you bought British government bonds in the early 1970s you would have had to wait over a decade, until the mid-1980s, just to recover the starting value of your capital in real terms; and even this only holds true on the assumption that you are not a taxpayer. If you are not a tax-exempt investor then government bonds can *never* provide protection against inflation.

This simple truth is emblematic of a deeper and more general one, and one that seems extremely difficult for most investors to accept. Liquidity is an expensive commodity; it always comes at a price.

While it is impossible to prove this mathematically, not least because it would involve much subjective input into the assessment of exactly what 'liquidity' was, and to what extent various assets possessed it, it seems logical to suggest that there is probably a more-or-less direct correlation here. The more liquid an asset is, the more expensive it is likely to be to hold it within your portfolio, and the less liquid, then the less expensive. As two asset types that might occupy the extreme ends of the continuum, one could perhaps nominate a US Treasury bill (or T-bill) as the 'very liquid' example, and an interest in a private equity fund as the 'very illiquid' example.

Such a view requires both explanation and justification. Surely the cost to an investor of holding a US Treasury instrument is some nominal dealing fee, whereas the cost of investing in a private equity fund, even if one ignores the legal and due diligence expenses at the outset, is an annual management fee which may be as much as 2 per cent of committed capital? Well, the answer as so often is 'Yes, but...'.

Yes, but this only takes into account the investor's direct expenses, what we might call their 'out of pocket' expenses. This does not offer a complete view of the situation. We must also take into account the investor's opportunity cost.

The 'cost' of investing in one thing is the cost of not investing in something else. Let us suppose that we have to choose between two investments, Asset A and Asset B. If we choose Asset A, but Asset B turns out to out-perform it by 10 per cent, then by choosing Asset A we have effectively made a loss of 10 per cent. In such a case, a benefit we could have enjoyed by choosing one alternative is a cost of having chosen the other alternative. Even though this idea was put forward over a century ago by the great Austrian economist Friedrich von Wieser, it still seems to be little understood in practice.

Why is this important? Because of something called the illiquidity premium. As we noted above, most investors are instinctively drawn to liquidity. Why, then, should they ever invest in something that is *not* liquid? There is only one possible answer to this: because they have an expectation of receiving higher long-term returns from an illiquid asset than they would expect from a liquid asset. If you think about it, any other explanation would be illogical. They see this higher expected return as the compensation to them for having given up some element of liquidity. If they did not expect a higher return then choosing an illiquid asset in the first place would be irrational.

Sophisticated investors, such as David Swensen, who has for many years run the Yale Endowment, have long since spotted that this means liquidity is a relatively expensive thing to buy. It comes at a price, in the shape of lower returns. The higher long-term returns that might be achieved by choosing an illiquid asset, less the return actually achieved on the liquid one, is the cost of the liquidity. In fact, slightly confusingly, people are now starting to talk about a liquidity premium, meaning specifically this higher price that investors are prepared to pay for liquidity. This is, of course, effectively the same thing as the illiquidity premium, since the higher return on illiquidity is the same thing as the cost of liquidity, but the terms can be perplexing, since it seems instinctive that they should mean the opposite of each other, rather than be synonymous.

So, because liquidity is expensive, it should be viewed as a luxury item to be bought and used as sparingly as possible. Yet, for most investors, it seems to be seen instead as a necessity that must be bought in great quantities regardless of the price. This mistaken view of liquidity is one of the greatest stumbling blocks to overcome when progressing the investment strategy process, particularly since many investors have been indoctrinated systematically for years, or even decades, by the likes of pension regulators and consultants. Yet, unless and until it can be overcome, it simply is not possible to take things further.

It follows that there should be as little liquidity as possible in a portfolio. To be clear, there may be some situations where 'as little as possible' is 100 per cent, but these will be very few and far between. It is almost impossible to conceive of an investor who has no need whatever to earn a return. Perhaps if you are a pension fund that is fully funded (or at least that is what the actuaries tell you) and whose youngest member is aged about 95 might qualify, but it really would have to be something as extreme as that.

It is up to every individual investor to decide the amount of liquidity required. With short-term investors, this might quite validly be a very large proportion of the total asset value. With long-term investors, it is a useful discipline, as suggested above, simply to decide how many years' liabilities you wish to cover, and set this amount aside in a liquidity pot that is kept constantly topped up. You can then be comfortable that, if necessary, you do not need any liquidity at all in the remainder in your long-term portfolio.

If you were to follow this argument to its logical conclusion, then, of course, you would not have any liquidity in your portfolio at all, but this is unlikely to be the case, for a couple of different reasons.

First, it is actually quite difficult to find assets that are totally illiquid. Even real estate assets and interests in infrastructure and private equity funds (with a few exceptions) can be disposed of within, say, three to six months if you are determined to do so and do not care about obtaining the highest possible price. Ironically, since many investors saw these as somehow being liquid, at least prior to mid-2007, it is interests in hedge funds that can be the most illiquid. Some have 'lock-ups' that may be as long as two years. Whatever the case, there must always be some element of liquidity within a long-term portfolio, even if it is not daily. It may well be, however. Unless you are a very large investor, you are likely to seek real estate exposure through real estate investment trusts (REITs), and other types of exposure through exchange-traded funds (ETFs), and these have daily liquidity just like any other quoted equities.

Second, remember that you need to top up your liquidity pot every quarter by adding on the liabilities of the next quarter (which is furthest out into the future) as the liabilities of the present quarter are discharged. This means that you must at any given time have within your long-term portfolio at least three-month liquidity in respect of at least one quarter's liabilities. As noted in the previous paragraph, this is unlikely to pose any difficulty provided you have a properly diverse asset mix.

Volatility

A detailed discussion of the nature of financial risk lies beyond the scope of this book. Suffice it to say that volatility and risk are not the same thing, but that for reasons which remain obscure most of the investment world chooses to treat them as if they are. The only one that makes any sense at all is that the mathematicians who came to dominate the financial world from the 1950s onwards were desperate for something they could calculate, and the variance of past periodic returns seemed like the best candidate.

Yet even this only 'makes sense' if you believe it is acceptable to substitute a question you can answer for one you cannot. One, moreover, which will produce a number that is guaranteed to be wrong, yet which will be endorsed enthusiastically as the one right answer. On this rather shabby confidence trick rests the whole of so-called modern portfolio theory (MPT).

It would be possible to write an entire book on this topic alone, but let us simply note the point now and move on. Since it is the way in which most investors (and, more important, their advisers) choose to think, then we must understand the concept even though we cannot accept it. We are in the position of atheists, say, who are none the less required to learn the Bible for a divinity exam.

Along with the obsession with often unnecessary levels of liquidity, the equation of risk with volatility is the second big stumbling block to the strategic process, since it means that the unenlightened, who are the majority, are like racehorses wearing blinkers. As we noted in Chapter 3, they are able to glimpse only a very narrow and constrained view of the world, rather than to see and appreciate the full landscape.

This mistaken thinking has various important consequences. Let us be aware in particular of three of the main ones. First, those who believe in volatility-as-risk will always seek to calculate a 'risk adjusted' rate of return using straightforward mean variance analysis with standard deviation (the square root of variance) as its chosen measure. Yet to conduct such an analysis requires the use of periodic returns. There is actually a strong argument (which is, needless to say, entirely ignored by the world of finance) that periodic returns may not be a valid measure of the cost or benefit to an investor of holding an investment, particularly over a long period, but let that go. More important still is the fact that, in respect of various asset types periodic returns can *never* be a valid measure. This applies in particular to asset types that exhibit long-term streams of cash flow in one or both directions, notably private equity and infrastructure funds, oil and gas royalties, and various types of real estate investment. For these, measures of compound return over time, such as an internal rate of return (IRR), need to be employed.

There is a particularly puzzling element to all of this, since finance theory recognises openly that the asset type which exhibits these characteristics most openly, namely bonds, should indeed be treated in this way rather than using annual returns. The yield to maturity of a bond is the same thing as its anticipated IRR, assuming that it was bought today and its purchase price treated as an initial negative cash flow. For the same reason, a different measure of risk is permitted, namely the risk that the issuer of the bond will at some stage default on its obligations on or before its maturity date (which, incidentally, is a very sensible measure).

Yet, if one attempts to move beyond bonds, then the shutter of this little window of sanity slams shut. While they may be happy to stuff their portfolio with bonds, many investors simply refuse to consider any other asset types for which periodic returns are not a good measure (or may not even be available), branding these 'alternative', and expressing surprise that anyone would be prepared to talk about these in polite society when it is not possible to calculate a 'risk-adjusted' return.

Thus, having chosen the wrong sort of box to delineate risk in the first place, investors reject any type of investment which they cannot fit into that box. So the first consequence of volatility-as-risk is that it artificially limits the scope of possible assets from which an investor can choose. Of course, if it happens to be illiquid as well, then its prospects are doubly cursed.

The second consequence of volatility-as-risk is that volatility, or rather restricting or limiting volatility, can very easily come to be seen as an end in itself. Ironically, many hedge funds, which are routinely seen by the media and the public at large as being 'high risk' investments, are actually marketed on precisely this basis. Far from increasing risk, they promise to limit it. Provided, of course, that you believe that risk and volatility are the same thing, and are so frightened of it that you are prepared to reduce your returns by paying a hefty fee to an investment manager to make some of the fear go away.

Thus it is commonplace to hear both investors and advisers speaking at conferences about constructing portfolios (usually composed of only bonds and equities) that will deliver a certain level of return within a certain number of standard deviations. Yet frequently such an approach may represent exactly the opposite of what the investor should be doing to achieve an optimal result. Since they are taught to view volatility as 'risk', and risk as being unwelcome, there is an instinctive view among investors that this 'risk' must necessarily be a bad thing, to be avoided at all costs. Yet because volatility is not actually 'risk' at all, the reality is that, as we shall see, volatility can actually be a good thing to be sought out, rather than a bad thing to be avoided.

The third consequence of volatility-as-risk is perhaps the most pernicious of all. Financial theory teaches, or at least assumes, that by calculating the standard deviation of the historical periodic returns of an asset or asset type you are assessing all its material risk. After all, if this were not the case, then why do it in the first place, why treat the output as the 'one right answer', and why use it as your exclusive aid to investment decision-making? If there was risk that lay outside the mean-variance process, other risk, perhaps even whole other *types* of risk, then the dogma of volatility-as-risk would lose its intellectual impregnability, and, as Dorothy Parker said, you can't teach an old dogma new tricks.

So investors who believe that volatility-as-risk is the complete answer are likely to put themselves in a very dangerous position. They will sit back contentedly, secure in the knowledge that they have worked out the risk of their portfolio to the last decimal point. They may even have used VaR (value at risk) techniques to calculate the maximum amount of money they might 'lose' (this includes unrealised losses) in any one day. Yet VaR uses exclusively mean-variance analysis.

Such investors may well be hit shortly afterwards by some cataclysmic event, perhaps even by some long-term systemic shift that completely shatters the cosy assumption that the past is a perfect mirror of the future, or that normal distribution (on which mean-variance analysis relies) always applies to investment outcomes. They will gaze, traumatised, at their statistical risk analysis, unable to understand what has happened.

The explanation will be simple, yet those who believe in volatility-as-risk will never be able to grasp it. Volatility is a dial on the investor's dashboard. It may be a very important dial, but it is only one of many, and it is most definitely not the same thing as risk.

How should investors view volatility?

For a short-term investor, volatility is definitely a bad thing. Remember, a short-term portfolio does not really contain 'investments' in the sense of assets that are selected with a view to increasing capital value, but rather instruments which are designed to be convertible into cash quickly, easily and reliably. So, as well as certainty that your piece of paper can indeed be turned into cash at any time you choose, you also want certainty of the *amount* of money it will generate. There is no point in buying an instrument for £100 only to find that when you need to turn it back into cash its market price has dropped to £90. The position of a short-term investor, or a short-term portfolio, can be summarised very neatly and it fits exactly the traditional view: liquidity good, volatility bad.

In fact, even so, a short-term investor will often be subject to significant volatility without realising it. As we have seen, the risk of bonds is, sensibly, viewed as the risk of possible default, and thus a prime government bond, which is assumed to have no default risk at all (a dangerous assumption) is held to be a 'risk-free' asset, which in turn generates a risk-free return. However, investors, God bless them, freely mix and match these two completely different types of risk, seemingly blissfully unaware that they are comparing apples with oranges.

Prime government bonds *may* be risk free in the sense of default risk (though almost certainly they are not) but they are certainly not risk free in the sense of volatility-as-risk. Because the yield of fixed-rate bonds goes up and down with financial market conditions and government policy, and this can only be effected by the market price of bonds going up or down in the opposite direction. In fact, viewed in isolation, bond prices turn out to be quite highly volatile – yet another unappreciated consequence of the myth of volatility-as-risk.

So we are happy to agree with the traditional view of volatility as an undesirable thing in so far as short-term portfolios are concerned, but what about their long-term counterparts? Here it can be argued strongly that things switch around and volatility becomes a desirable thing, something investors should be chasing, not avoiding.

This may at first sight appear to be built around a paradox. Investors seek to make a gain, to achieve and maximise their investment return. Yet markets go down as well as up. So, in seeking a gain they must also necessarily accept the possibility of incurring a loss instead. If this is the case, why should investors want their portfolio to exhibit more volatility rather than less?

The answer lies in what volatility (or variance to use its fancy statistical name) captures. It effectively measures the extent to which an asset or a market goes both up and down on either side of the average, or mean. Something with high volatility is likely to go both up and down a long way, while something with low volatility will travel only a short distance away from the mean, whether it is up or down.

Now let's turn our attention to something like the stock market. As we know, this goes up or down on any single day. It may go down for a number of days in a row, or even for several years in a row, but it is not going to go down for ever. Sooner or later it is going to start to go back up again. In fact, viewed since about 1996, an index such as the Dow Jones seems to resemble three rather jagged mountains as it has gone up and down in what some argue have been three discernible cycles.

Whatever the case, the words 'sooner or later' are important. A long-term investor can wait for that 'sooner or later' and ride the market back up again. You see, another important difference between a long-term investor and a short-term one is that a long-term investor need never be a forced seller of any asset, whereas a short-term investor almost certainly will be at some stage. Provided you can afford to wait, if you are looking to have as lengthy an upward ride as possible, surely you would prefer to be starting your journey from the second floor rather than from the sixth? In which case, you should embrace volatility rather than fear it.

There are two important provisos here. The first is that we are talking about stock markets, not individual company stocks. There may actually be a very good reason why an individual stock is going down, and it may indeed go all the way down to zero, whereas this can never happen in the case of an entire market, since as an individual stock drops out of the index it will be replaced by the next in line.

The second is that it does *not* assume that you are clairvoyant, and can spot exactly the right time to buy back into the market. On the contrary, it assumes that you will have chosen a number of different asset types and will be rebalancing between them on a regular basis. You do not need to be a mathematical genius to spot that if the prices of various assets are the same at the end of a period as they were at the beginning of it, but that you have rebalanced between them as they went up and down in the meantime, then you will have made money. Nor is it difficult to grasp that the greater the extent to which they have gone up and down during the period, then the greater the overall gain you will have made. So, for a long-term investor, whose imperative is to make a return rather than to be able to turn assets instantly into cash, volatility is actually a highly desirable thing. All you need to be able to do is to hold your nerve and not be panicked into selling something just because it has gone down in price, something, sadly, that many investors seem unable to resist.

So this question of whether you are a long- or short-term investor or, more likely, to what extent you are a mixture of each, is of fundamental importance and needs to be addressed at a very early stage of the strategic process. At the same time, the facilitator needs to try to clear the mental clutter that surrounds the concepts of liquidity and volatility. Patiently and repeatedly asking 'Why?' every time someone claims to need liquidity or avoid volatility can only be helpful. Another technique which can be quite effective is to say 'I think you mean volatility' every time someone mentions 'risk'.

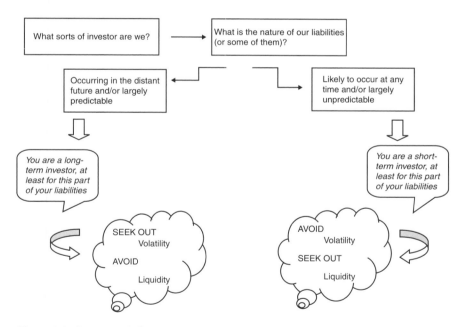

Figure 4.1 Long- and short-term investors: what sorts of liabilities do we have?

5
SWOT Analysis for Investors

Just about every reader will be familiar with the concept of SWOT analysis, with SWOT standing for the four categories into which issues that are identified during the strategic process can be split:

- Strengths
- Weaknesses
- Opportunities
- Threats

The first two listed are internal. They relate to aspects of the organisation in question, and act to place it either at some advantage or disadvantage, respectively. We shall be devoting the rest of this chapter to identifying the sorts of things that investors should consider during this inward-facing analysis.

The second pair – opportunities and threats – are external. They relate to the environment within which the organisation has to function, including both macro factors and the actions, both actual and potential, of third parties. This can be a difficult and emotive area to probe. Just as many businesses find it difficult to accept that they have true competitors, so many organisations seem to think it is a sign of weakness to admit that there may be adverse circumstances beyond their control (though they may plan to lessen their consequences). We shall, however, defer consideration of this outward-facing analysis to Chapter 6.

Strengths and weaknesses

This can also be a difficult area to probe. We like to think that all our qualities are positive and desirable, hence the often-encountered interview question 'What are your weaknesses, do you think?' to which, incidentally, 'I don't think I have any' is absolutely the wrong answer.

There are two possible approaches to this. One is to let everyone stare dreamily into the distance and suggest individual factors that might qualify in either camp. However, a more structured approach will usually pay greater dividends. A good facilitator will move the discussion through a number of specific areas and see what emerges from each. Normally it should be evident, perhaps after a little Socratic dialogue with the facilitator, what should go into each box, but there may occasionally be situations where different subjective assessments are at variance. They can agree on the facts, but not on whether they are a good or a bad thing for the organisation. These should be listed as issues, to be returned to in due course once some other parts of the picture have been sketched in. Like a crossword, it can be easier to resolve some questions once you can see how their answers might fit into the overall scheme of things.

The choice of topics will differ from one investor to another. A small wealth management team will hardly have the same way of doing things as a large sovereign wealth fund. However, they will cover broadly the same issues. Let us set out the main areas for discussion.

Before we do so, however, a word of caution, or rather two words. First, whether something is a strength or a weakness will depend to a large extent on what investors are trying to achieve. Are they a long-term or a short-term investor? Are they looking to invest domestically or globally? Trying to lock in liquidity, chasing returns or seeking to preserve capital? Second, to assume that you know the answer to these questions presupposes that you have already been through the part of the process we have covered previously, and have come up with some honest and thoughtful answers.

The failure to do so is one of the most common shortcomings of the process as a whole. Many investors who do recognise the necessity of conducting a strategic process sit down to embark on it honestly believing that SWOT analysis is the right place to start. For some types of strategy, such as mainstream corporate strategy, this can often be true because issues such as 'Who are we?' and 'What do we do?' have been considered for so long that they have become an accepted part of the group consciousness.

Yet even here danger can lurk. There is the well-known story of a new CEO arriving at the Parker Pen company and asking his first board meeting who was their most direct competitor. 'Sheaffer', proffered one director. The CEO shook his head. 'Waterman' suggested another. Another shake of the head. The answer, he told them, was Ronson. They needed to stop thinking about themselves as being manufacturers of writing implements and realise that they were instead in the market of prestige and usually one-off gifts given mainly to men. Thus they competed at least as much with the makers of expensive cigarette lighters as they did with other pen companies. (This is a story, needless to say, from an earlier and more tobacco-friendly age.)

By far the most important of these preliminary questions, however, is 'What sort of investor are we?' in the sense of long- or short-term, which is why this topic has already been covered separately. As we have seen, the answer for most investors is that they will be a mix of each, with a corresponding mix of assets. It is against this backdrop that internal factors fall to be considered. Something that is a weakness for a long-term investor may not be so for a short-term investor, and vice versa.

Let us look at some of the most important aspects of the organisation that will need to be considered. Incidentally, just about all of these will be capable of change, though the degree of difficulty in effecting such change may vary enormously.

Decision-making

Most investors are loath to admit that their own internal procedures can be a weakness, yet in many cases this is undeniably the case, in which case the organisation needs to decide whether to change these, or to plan to work within them to maximum advantage – or, more correctly, minimum disadvantage.

To a large extent this factor will be driven by who makes those decisions. As a general rule, the further away in organisational terms from the people who actually work at the coalface of day-to-day investment are such decisions made, the slower (always) and less efficient (usually) will be the process. This is in part a procedural phenomenon and in part one of expertise.

Boards or Committees work best when they discuss and set investment strategy, leaving tactical and operational matters to the functional specialists. However, this is a counsel of perfection that is rarely met in practice. It is much more likely in real life that the board or committee will throw itself into the minutiae of manager selection and monitoring, for which it frequently possesses neither the time nor the expertise to do properly. To make matters even worse, this will usually be after little or no strategic discussion (since all the available time is required for tactical matters), and thus in a random and haphazard fashion; it is driven by micro-events rather than within the framework of a rational strategy which has been clearly agreed and communicated.

It is necessary to be very dispassionate in considering procedures, perhaps drawing up an organisational chart and a flow diagram of the investment decision process. Perhaps the most common, and also sadly the worst, will go something like that described below.

An interesting fund proposal will arrive and, having lain around in someone's in-tray for a month or two, will eventually be discussed by the investment team, at which point someone will say 'But we don't have an allocation for this', which will usually be the end of it.

Assuming that it is not, the CIO might mention the fund in guardedly favourable terms at the next board meeting, and ask for permission to put up a discussion paper on whether the organisation should have an allocation to this asset type after all. At this point there will usually be dark mutterings from the consultant at the end of the table, pointing out that it if this was a good idea then the consultant's own firm would already have suggested it and they haven't, so it isn't. Again, this will usually be the end of the matter.

Let us assume for the sake of argument that this hurdle can be overcome. The next board agenda might already be so full of important things that cannot possibly be shifted (such as interviewing the several bond managers already appointed) that it might have to be held over to the next meeting. By now it is quite possible that six months or more might already have elapsed. During this period, incidentally, the chairman may well tell the CIO that the consultants have had a word with him in confidence to express their concerns, and ask the CIO to quietly drop the whole idea.

At the next board meeting, the consultant will take up most of the ten minutes or so allocated for discussion of the matter by saying repeatedly that this would be a very high risk course of action, without, of course, ever actually explaining what they mean by 'risk'. Seeing the board members glancing doubtfully at each other, the chairman will either put the matter to the vote, at which point it will be rejected, or ask the consultant's own firm to produce a paper, showing, naturally, the 'risk adjusted' returns any such decision would have produced if made a decade or so previously.

At the next board meeting the consultant will produce a report that consists largely of tables of industry returns of dubious origin, damn the asset type with faint praise, making free with various letters of the Greek alphabet in the process, and conclude by saying dismissively that in any event the particular fund manager concerned does not appear in their in-house database.

Should there be any board members left who are still in favour of an allocation, a further complication may arise in the case of European public sector investors. The chairman will remind them that they are subject to the EU tendering regulations and are not free merely to go out and appoint investment managers as they wish. They must instead initiate an arcane exercise that involves putting a notice in the *Official Journal of the European Union* (OJEU), which does not feature on the reading list of anyone in the investment community, and waiting a certain number of days, within which any fund manager who wishes to be considered has to put in a tender (in the right form, naturally).

By now, something between 18 months and two years may well have passed. There only remains a lengthy process of interviews and discussions with your consultants, sign-off by your lawyers and SRI[1] team, and reporting back to the board, which even if everything goes strictly to plan is likely to take another six months or so. Needless to say, the original fund manager who sparked this convoluted decision process has long since closed its fund, so that the decision no longer has any meaning in any case.

If you recognise all, or even some of, this as being a fair, though somewhat mischievous description of the way in which your organisation takes decisions, you have a serious problem and can only possibly brand your investment process itself as a strategic weakness.

At the other extreme, a comprehensive strategic process will have been undertaken, as a result of which everyone will know to which areas they have allocations, and why. There will also have been discussions regarding how each of these areas is to be accessed, and any limitations that should apply in each area. Decision-making within these parameters will then be delegated to a sub-committee consisting in each case of the professional team actually responsible for these investments. Such systems work well. I was personally involved in one situation in which an investment was taken from proposal to completion in six weeks, even allowing for full due diligence and legal input.

We shall see when we come to consider active and passive investment how the nature of the decision process, and specifically the amount of time that the board or committee has available to it, should itself be an important factor in deciding the organisation's overall investment approach. Yet this can only work if the organisation is totally honest with itself about exactly what that process is, and how it operates in practice.

Regulatory constraints

In the previous section we saw an example of regulatory constraints on investor freedom of action, namely the dreaded OJEU requirements, to whose strictures public sector investors such as pension funds may have

---

1. Socially responsible investing.

been surprised to find themselves subject, since some have suggested that they were aimed primarily at stopping continental officials from granting the supply contract for their departmental toilet paper needs to their brothers-in-law.

There are, however, many others, including those governing pension funds in Scandinavia, the Netherlands and the UK. Not content with this, the European Union (EU) is proposing to extend the Solvency II rules that currently govern insurance companies to pension funds across Europe. Similarly, the Basel III accords (more extreme versions of which are being proposed by the UK and Switzerland) find governments setting out what sorts of assets (yes, you've guessed it, government bonds) need to be held by banks against Tier 1 capital. In other words, for many organisations, investment choice has all but disappeared. Asset allocation is driven not by possible investment return, but by regulation.

All of which is a sad reflection on the sort of society we have decided to live in, or more precisely that which those we have elected have decided we should be forced to live in. However, it is no part of this book to seek to propose more sensible arrangements. This work is intended as a practical handbook dealing with reality as it is rather than as we would like it to be. However, it is surely valid to reflect in passing on the zeal and enthusiasm with which governments, both national and federal, are busily suppressing freedom, and the lack of concern this seems to be arousing in the investment community, where apathy and fatalism seem to constitute the prevailing emotional state. One is reminded of words attributed to Edmund Burke – namely that all that is necessary for evil to flourish is that good men should do nothing.

Dealing with reality as it is, however, it is necessary that you have a very clear idea of exactly what you are allowed to do, and how. There is no point in coming up with some highly intelligent strategic approach if it is not one you can legally execute. Nor should you simply look at the regulations. In some cases, particularly with investors who are public bodies, their constitutional documents will also have a part to play.

Expertise

In perhaps no other area do investors differ from each other than in the degree of expertise enjoyed by their staff. You will frequently hear certain investors being described as 'sophisticated'. In some circumstances this can be a term of legal significance, but in practice it can be taken more generally to have reference to the amount of financial knowledge and experience to which they have access internally, and in particular to expertise in specialist asset areas such as hedge funds, private equity, infrastructure and so on.

At one end of the scale may be found large investors who have a specialist team for each asset type, while at the other end may be found pension funds who do not employ a single investment professional.

Obviously, this will be a major factor in setting asset allocation decisions. The old adage 'Don't invest in things you don't understand' is one of the soundest ever uttered. It is clearly desirable that there should be as close a relationship as possible between the areas of expertise of an investor's staff and the types of assets in which they choose to invest. As we shall see later when we consider active and passive investing, lack of expertise should not be a total stumbling block, but in many cases it will be, and the three asset types mentioned above would be good examples.

Expertise is, of course, an area directly under the organisation's control. If the organisation decides to make an allocation to Asian real estate, an expert on Asian real estate could be hired but, particularly in the case of public sector investors, rigid and artificial pay scales can get in the way. So too can a failure to conduct a proper cost–benefit analysis, taking into account in particular the costs of proceeding in alternative ways. The cost of an in-house expert will almost always be less than the fees of an external gatekeeper or fund of funds manager.

In practice, one often finds lack of expertise being used as an excuse not to consider the full range of available asset types. Perhaps predictably, such cases frequently coincide with an unwillingness on the part of the board to delegate investment decisions to those best qualified to make them.

SRI, religious and ethical considerations

The mention of SRI earlier was not intended to be in any way facetious. Nobody who has lived through the events of the last decade or two could possibly deny that in many cases the practice of finance appears to have become divorced from social responsibility, nor that this is a deeply troubling and unwelcome state of affairs. Social responsibility matters, and many investors around the world now insist on SRI sign-off, whether internal or external, before finalising any investment decision.

It therefore seems only sensible to make sure that everyone in any way connected with the investment process should be made aware of key SRI issues and, more importantly, the ways in which these are likely to be interpreted and applied by one's own particular SRI team. Should a particular course of action be likely to be vetoed by them at the final decision stage, a great deal of time could be saved by not embarking upon it in the first place.

Religious issues can also come to the fore, particularly in the case of Islamic investors. Islamic law forbids the taking of interest and, depending on the view of individual investors, things such as alcohol, gambling and pork products can also raise issues. In much the same way, SRI may have problems with things like tobacco products and the arms trade. Most investment funds these days have special provisions in place to allow concerned investors to be excused from participating in such investments, but this does not entirely address things such as headline risk (see below).

Similarly, nobody would deny that today ethical issues are more relevant than ever in the practice of finance and investment, and the definition of 'ethical' is tricky, since it is a subjective, fluid and constantly evolving term. For example, some are now suggesting that certain type of fee arrangements or financial structures may themselves be 'unethical', regardless of what the underlying fund or transaction is designed to do. These issues should be fully and freely discussed within an organisation on a regular basis; investment strategy should not take place in an ethical vacuum.

As well as being comfortable that they are being ethical and socially responsible, many investors today are concerned today to *be seen* to be ethical. This gives rise to something called headline risk. A pension fund connected to the retail industry would not like to be named as an investor in a buyout fund which stands accused in the press of having driven a retail business into insolvency, regardless of whether the accusations are justified, and regardless of the fact that the pension fund had no part to play in the investment decision. Headline risk is driven by emotional, not logical, motives. Incidentally, this also washes across into purely financial considerations; understandably, no investor wants to be named as having participated in a failed hedge fund or a fraudulent investment scheme. Such factors can and do influence investment decision-making so, again, if the board is sensitive regarding certain areas it is sensible to request that these are made explicit in advance, rather than after several months' work has been carried out on a particular opportunity.

Opportunities and threats

These require consideration of factors that are external to the organisation, things that are part of the wider environment within which the organisation operates. This definition, though it suffices in areas such as marketing and general corporate strategy, is a little sloppy when it comes to the business of investment, since, of course, things like legal and regulatory issues would qualify, and we have discussed them above under strengths and weaknesses. So it is probably better to add the rider 'and which themselves have no direct effect on the organisation's freedom of choice'.

Of course, the possibility of a new regulation, perhaps which has been discussed but not yet framed, *is* a threat, and sadly one that needs increasingly to be planned for.

Another way of thinking about it is that opportunities and threats are features on the map on which you plan your journey, but strengths and weaknesses are what determine your mode of transport. To pursue this analogy a little further, the opportunities and threats are a little like the ladders and snakes in the famous board game. So far as possible, you should be looking to take advantage of the opportunities and planning how best to deal with the threats should they in fact transpire.

Incidentally, the technique of scenario planning, which we met earlier, will necessarily involve the identification of opportunities and threats before deciding how likely it is that each will arise, whether or not in combination with others and, in any case, the extent of its likely impact.

In investment terms. some of these external forces are fairly obvious, other less so.

Inflation

Inflation is a clear threat to all investors. It is fundamental that one must at least preserve the value of one's capital in real terms even if one is not actually going to grow it, though not so fundamental that at the time of writing, this is being ignored by investors all over the world who are electing to hold government bonds that are generating a negative real yield. In fact, it is such a clear threat that many investors are starting to treat this as an 'exposure' to which they are subject, and plan specific portfolios to try to mitigate its effects. We shall discuss this exposure based approach later.

However, different levels of inflation should be modelled as part of the scenario planning exercise. I have referred in other books to inflation as the mouse in the larder that is permanently nibbling away, so that sooner or later all the food the larder contains will disappear. John Maynard Keynes saw it rather as a secret tax, which steadily transfers wealth from the individual to the state. Whatever the case, if you do nothing then the value of your capital *must* fall. At times of high inflation, the effects can become frightening. Within living memory in the UK, retail prices doubled in eleven years.[2]

---

2. From 1969. See Office of National Statistics, retail price inflation data.

For investors who are allowed to gear themselves with debt, inflation brings an extra dimension to planning. During periods of high inflation it is actually advantageous to be a borrower, since one ends up paying back the debt to the lender with devalued money. This is why governments like inflation so much, so long as it doesn't run out of control and risk causing electoral unpopularity. However, this will in turn open up all sorts of other issues for consideration. For one thing, personal borrowing is not usually available on the same sort of extended time scale as it is for governments. For another, interest payments place extra stress on the investor's cash-flow modelling. Whatever the case, and whatever the outcome, the discussion at least needs to take place.

Longevity

Since longevity too can be planned for as part of an exposure-based system, it probably belongs alongside inflation for our present purposes. Life expectancy is obviously a particular problem for pension funds, for whom the risk of their members living longer than anticipated translates into extra payments of benefits that have not been budgeted. Again, this is considered separately later in the book.

Sponsor risk

While considering pension funds it is worth mentioning sponsor risk, a risk, it has to be said, that many pension funds – particularly in the UK – entirely failed to deal with until it was too late to do anything effective about it. In part this was because of the obvious conflicts of interest inherent in having directors of the company also sitting as trustees of the pension fund. 'Obvious' to everyone except the British government, that is, since it has been public policy in the UK not just to encourage this but actually to enforce it.

Occupational pension funds rely on three sources of funding. Most obviously there is the gain they make on their investment activities, so much so that some consultants refer to the risk of losing money as 'investment risk' as far as pension trustees are concerned, but it is submitted that this is both a very clumsy approach and a particularly unhelpful one. Clumsy in so far as there are different elements of investment risk, which can and should be split out and considered separately as part of the strategic process; and unhelpful in that it seems to suggest that this is a risk where trustees in some way have a choice as to whether they take it or not, whereas, of course, they do not, or at least they should not if they are doing their jobs properly.

The other two sources of funding are, first, contributions from members (by way of deductions from their salaries); and, second, from the employer, or sponsor. It is in the latter that sponsor risk is to be found.

Put simply, it is the risk of the sponsor proving financially unable to make contributions at some stage. This risk is actually much more severe than it might seem, for not only does the sponsor have to make regular contributions in the same way as the members of the scheme (its employees), it may also from time to time be called upon to make lump sum payments to top up the capital value of the fund's assets.

So, consideration of the financial health of the sponsor must form a key part of the strategic planning process of an occupational pension fund. How likely is it that the sponsor will be able to make the regular contributions that have already been budgeted? How likely is it that supplemental payments will be required, and that the sponsor will be able to honour such requests? The situation may be complicated, in countries where this is permitted, by the sponsor threatening to close the final salary scheme completely if such requests are made.

No matter how difficult it may be because of the inherent conflicts of interest, the trustees must conduct the exercise via the perspective of a creditor of the company. If approached in the right sprit on both sides, inventive solutions may be found. For example, in some cases the sponsor has transferred its real estate assets to the fund and then leased them back. In others, ways have been found of granting the scheme security over the sponsor's assets, or some of them, to provide partial protection in the event of the company becoming insolvent.

Counterparty risk

Until the autumn of 2007 nobody paid much attention to counterparty risk. Certain banks and other corporations, and many governments, were deemed to carry effectively no default risk at all, so that anybody would be happy to accept, say, a German government bond as a risk free asset. Similarly, most investors would have viewed a corporate bond issued by the likes of Deutsche Bank or Coca-Cola as, while not technically being 'risk free', something pretty close to that.

This was perhaps fortunate for those who were issuing or holding derivative instruments such as swaps and options, since they did not have to worry about the possibility of their counterparty being unable to pay out when the time came to honour their obligations. Of course, they were wrong, but just how tragically wrong only became clear as the events of 2008 unfolded. Lehman Brothers, for example, had issued many derivative instruments.

This risk has to some extent been mitigated, and continues to be so, in respect of derivatives by a continuing shift, driven by regulation, away from 'OTC' instruments and towards those that are issued and settled through a recognised exchange. 'OTC' stands for 'over the counter', which is a rather misleading term in that it originally meant a specific matched-bargain way of trading securities. In its more current usage it means those that are issued directly by one counterparty to another, rather than those that involve the intervention of an exchange or clearing house. In the former case, the party entitled to payment takes the risk of their counterparty's insolvency, and in the latter case, the exchange itself would pay out, using funds taken from all issuers by way of security. Of course, there is still the risk that in abnormal market conditions these funds, and any supplemental calls, would prove unequal to the task, but this risk is clearly minimal when compared with what we might call naked counterparty risk.

Counterparty risk remains an issue with OTC instruments, however. Why do these still exist, when the alternative seems so attractive? Because exchanges require standardisation of both term and amount, and so where an investor such as a pension fund is looking for a 'made to measure' solution to hedge a particular perceived risk they may be forced to accept OTC instruments.

A much larger problem concerns bonds. Here there is no guarantee of any kind, simply a contractual obligation to repay ('redeem') the bond on its maturity and to pay an agreed level of income ('coupon') in the meantime. Again, pre-2007 this was not felt to be too great a concern, but it has subsequently become a very obvious one, given the downgrading of many nations' credit ratings and outright default by others.

It would seem a logical suggestion to advance that investors should seek to diversify this risk away whenever possible; for example, by holding bonds from a wide variety of different issuers, both government and corporate, well spread between different geographies and industrial sectors. Perversely, however, the period post-2007 has in many cases seen a greater concentration of issuer risk than ever before. In particular, many investors now hold very high amounts of the debt of their own government, as a result of political pressure, intellectual cowardice, and in some cases even coercion (in the shape of regulation or direct government control).

The argument against spreading your net more widely is, in many cases, currency. If your liabilities are in, say, euros, then does it really make sense to hold assets that may be denominated in dollars, yen or sterling? Surely you then have a currency risk, which you did not have before? Well, yes you do, but you are trading one risk off against another. So the discussion should not be about whether you wish to take on more risk, but about which types of risk you are prepared to accept, and in what proportions. Sadly, the ongoing myth of prime government bonds being 'risk free' assets means that this issue is rarely identified, let alone discussed.

This is a situation that needs to addressed, and urgently. The sad truth is that, in a post-2007 environment, any issuer, no matter how seemingly sound (and how many are even that?), can default, and the possibility of such default should form part of scenario planning. To have all your counterparty eggs in one basket must surely be extremely rash.

Government action

There is a natural tendency to assume that others think as you do; this is actually a well-recognised cognitive bias, as has already been pointed out. Similarly, there seems to be an equally irrational tendency to believe that government is enlightened and benign, and will always behave in a reasonable and legal manner. This can have the effect of blinding investors to threats they need to consider, but don't.

In recent years, government actions have included forcing through bank mergers which would have been ruled unlawful if attempted by corporations themselves (UK); the giving of state aid to banks on preferential terms, which is nominally illegal under EU law (UK); legalised theft from bank shareholders (UK); determined efforts to prevent investors from holding gold instead of government bonds (Netherlands); the imposition of arbitrary bans on short selling, illegal under EU law (France and Germany); theft from public funds (Ireland); theft from private savings accounts (Argentina); theft through forced nationalisation (Argentina again); retrospective legislation to void land purchases by foreign investors (Brazil); the creation through regulation and quantitative easing of a false market in their own securities (most governments around the world); and a tax on inflation (UK).

It should be apparent from this that government is not benign at all. On the contrary, it represents a huge threat to investors' interests, as does central bank policy. So much so, in fact, that some respected investment managers are talking openly about trying to keep their clients' assets as far away as possible from the effect of government action and central bank policy. Wise investors would do well to consider this point for themselves.

Of course, the degree of urgency with which you do so will be driven in part by your view of the likely outcomes of the current crisis, as embodied within your scenario modelling, but there are many simple steps you might be able to take with only modest cost implications. Perhaps you might be able to make some investments directly, rather than through managers who may be subject to regulatory pressure? Could you move the physical custody of your assets to independent countries outside the United States or the European Union? Might you even be able to move your whole organisation to such a jurisdiction? These are the sorts of issues you need to discuss.

You also need to have some contingency plans against specific events. For example, the British government is known to have emergency plans in place for a total capital lock-down in the event of major upheaval within the Eurozone. If you are a British investor and have not already discussed how this might affect you, and what you might do to forestall it, you are simply not doing your job properly.

Global macro

This is, of course, the name for a recognised hedge fund strategy, but all investors should be alive to the chance of events occurring on a macro level, and the possible implications for their own plans. It might be useful to think of the first three horsemen of the apocalypse: pestilence, war and famine, while the fourth (death) might exemplify natural disasters and terrorist attacks.

We saw pestilence, in the form of Asian bird flu, ravage the tourist trade in various parts of the world. What might be the effect of a sudden pandemic of a mutated flu strain to which there was currently no defence? War could take the form of North Korea attacking the South; or America, together with any country they can persuade to join them, attacking Iran. Famine could arise as a result of plant disease or drought. Death could be by tsunami or terrorist action.

These are frightening possibilities, but they must nevertheless be discussed. It may be that you have concluded that there is nothing you can do in practical terms about any of them, but you need at least to have the discussion.

Economic indicators

It may seem strange that this section has been left till last. After all, many investors read the economics pages of the financial press devotedly and have earnest discussions with their colleagues about the implications of the latest figures on US unemployment, or German factory gate prices. Yes, of course, these are important matters and any well-read investor should indeed be having these thoughts and conversations but, with the exception of inflation, which is a severe and ever-present threat to any investor's objectives, care should be exercised when attempting to incorporate economic modelling into your process.

The efficient market hypothesis tells us that the market price of any asset (or, as many investors are starting to say instead, of any risk) already has factored into it current expectations, both about that asset specifically (for example, the likely future earnings of a company whose shares you hold) and about the financial environment generally (for example, predicted inflation and interest rates). Thus, financial or economic forecasts are only really of any use to you as an investor if you *disagree* with them. If the market is factoring in that inflation in six months' time will be 3 per cent, but you believe it will be higher than that, then you might take a short position in bonds or interest rates, gambling that the government will raise interest rates to choke off inflationary pressures. There are other ways you could play this, of course, with inflation or interest rate swaps, or by going long on the currency, since it should rise with any unexpected rise in interest rates. Yet you would need to be pretty brave to do any of these, particularly as economic forecasts are often based on a bundle of individual forecasts or models, representing the consensus view.

The second problem is that, in fact, many economic forecasts *do* turn out to be wrong. Government bodies, in particular, seem to issue forecasts that are consistently too optimistic, only to have to scale them back retrospectively. However, by the time this is done a new set of figures has been released, upon which the market is now relying, and so, unless a particularly severe correction comes as too great a shock, the markets generally shrug off such news and press on.

The third leg of the problem is that, as mentioned above, taking advantage of perceived mis-forecasting is not necessarily an easy task. On the contrary, it can require quite sophisticated techniques that are well outside the day-to-day experience of mainstream investors. It can also call for a fairly rapid and decisive decision process, which, as we have seen, will rarely be present. Thus if an investor does want to play this particular area there is a strong argument for doing so through a few specialist hedge fund managers, perhaps particularly those who target currency using a 'value' approach, where they go long or short depending on their view of a currency's relative purchasing power, or the 'carry trade' where they are effectively taking a bet on how various interest rates will move relative to each other. Even so, there is no guarantee that they will get it right!

6
What Are We Trying to Achieve?

We have now looked at how we go about conducting the process, how we work out what kind of investor we are, and what sorts of issues, both internal and external, we should be taking into consideration. We might think of this as having worked out our present location on the map. We now need to agree on what our objectives might be, since unless and until we can fix our target destination, we shall simply be moving around aimlessly, no matter how good a map we have and no matter how expert we might be at interpreting it.

Remember what was said earlier in the book – that Napoleon commented that strategy marches in both time and space simultaneously. We therefore need to agree on not just what we are trying to achieve, but also over how long a period. We can translate this into investment terms by talking about our target rate of return on the one hand, and our investment time horizon on the other. In both cases, we should be having this discussion in the light of our liabilities, actual if possible (or at least actual as currently modelled, which is not quite the same thing), and assumed or adopted if not.

We touched on this earlier, but it is now time to look at it in detail. The important thing to understand as a starting point is that investment decision-making should not take place in a vacuum. Sadly, it is necessary to say 'should not' because in practice it often does. Worse still, it does not seem to occur to anybody to question this. Once again, the word 'Why' should come to our rescue: why do we invest?

Why do we invest?

Investing might be regarded as akin to saving in that it is an alternative use of money compared to going out and spending it. Indeed, for many very small potholders, such as pensioners putting a few pounds away each month, a savings account might be the only practicable form of investment available to them. Either way, we are talking about deferring spending, about choosing to reserve some money to spend in the future rather than today.

Again, the word 'Why?' Why should we do this? Why should we pass up the opportunity for instant gratification unless we have some specific alternative in mind? In other words, there is an opportunity cost to choosing to invest in the first place, just as there is to any choice made subsequently within the decision process. It may be that we have no say in the matter – for example, if we are a member of a pension fund and are having to contribute a fixed amount every month – but in just about every other case we *do* have a choice. We need to be clear about why we are prepared to bear this cost, and how much we are willing to pay.

It could be argued that, in the case of many private individuals, they are motivated simply by the idea of 'putting something away for a rainy day' and therefore have no specific objective in mind, but this can at best be only partly true. This motivation is driven by concerns that they will need to pay out amounts in the future, such as housing or health care costs, which they might not otherwise be able to afford. Thus they *are* thinking of future liabilities, but cannot specify how much these might be or when they might arise. Institutional investors can and should be much more scientific about this.

How and why should our investment goals be driven by our future liabilities?

And yet again, 'Why?'. Why should we look to model our future liabilities? Because by doing so we can work out what rate of return we need to make on our assets, both present and future, to be reasonably sure of being able to meet these liabilities as they occur. This becomes our target rate of return. Note the phrase 'as they occur'. We should *not* be concerned as to whether we can pay them, or even some artificial net present value (NPV) that allegedly represents them, now, today. We should be concerned about whether we are likely to be able to meet them as they arise in the future. Sadly, public policy towards pension funds in most countries takes the former view, fundamentally misguided though it obviously is, and this goes unchallenged by pension sponsors, trustees and consultants alike.

Pension funds are in the best position here, since they will be able to model their future liabilities as to both amount and duration. The former may be subject to the vagaries of inflation, but this can be dealt with by thinking in 'inflation plus' terms. The latter is only as good as your actuaries' judgement, which has traditionally been pretty poor, but this can be addressed by scenario modelling, flexing longevity as a variable. So, at least within certain limits, they can and should be able to model their liabilities quite easily.

In the case of final salary (defined benefit – DB) pension schemes, they will, however, model their situation rather differently depending on whether they are open or closed to new members. In the case of a scheme that is closed to new members and will therefore be wound up when the last remaining beneficiary dies, the capital of the scheme can be run down towards (but not quite reaching) zero as time goes by. In other words, the present net asset value (NAV) of the fund can be put towards future liabilities.

In the case of a scheme that is still open to new members, however, this would be a most unwise approach to adopt. Probably the prudent approach is to set as one's target the preservation in real terms, throughout the period modelled, of the present value of the portfolio. Incidentally, if you do model the situation on this basis you will appreciate at once just how challenging it is both to do this and to meet future liabilities, and why so many final salary schemes have closed.

A final point for consideration about final salary schemes is the period over which they can usefully model anything at all. As we all know, the further into the future events are listed to occur, then the greater the uncertainty of the outcome, and thus the greater the uncertainty factor that has to be introduced into the calculations (which might take the form either of a blanket percentage increase in longevity, period by period, or a premium over the calculated target return). At what point does this uncertainty become so great that the whole modelling process begins to lose its value? There are, for example, some pension schemes which model liabilities as much as 100 years into the future.

It is submitted that this is too much of a good thing. Better perhaps to model some more manageable period, say 25 years, but on a rolling basis, so that with each year that passes an additional year is added on to the end. If you are adopting the suggestion made a little earlier of aiming to preserve the inflation adjusted asset value constant across the period, then little harm can be done by this slightly truncated approach.

Life insurance companies have a slightly more complex task, since they will typically also be annuity providers and so longevity will affect both sides of their modelling, but as these two are a natural hedge against each other, this should in fact lead to less uncertainty than in the case of a pension fund. They will, however, need to consider carefully what assumptions they are going to make about the levels of new business of either type they are planning to write in the future, not least because their liabilities (annuities) may well be linked to inflation, whereas their assets (such as bonds) may not.

Many foundations are obliged to pay out a certain proportion of their asset value every year, and here the basic arithmetic will be simple. Less so the assumptions, which here risk becoming circular, because the investment objective to be chosen will affect the amount to be paid out, which in turn will have to be measured against the specific cost of certain projects which the Foundation may have agreed in advance to cover. Inflation, too, will have to be considered effectively as an extra cost; again, we come back to Keynes's view of inflation as a secret tax.

The important point to discuss with respect to inflation is how you wish to take it into account. Do you attempt to forecast the rate in future years and build this into calculating an overall target rate of return? Or do you ignore it and then take whatever target rate of return is calculated as being the excess required over the rate of inflation? Neither approach precludes attempting to fund ways of hedging inflation if you can, and this is dealt with elsewhere in the book.

College endowments may have agreed to contribute specific sums to the college budget for a certain number of years, so the college will at least be able to model these with some certainty, though obviously assumptions will need to be made thereafter. Some sort of annuity growth factor would seem to be a sensible starting point.

With investors such as family offices and sovereign wealth funds things become more complex as it may well not be possible for them to identify any specific future liabilities at all. The former could ask all beneficiaries to keep them updated regularly with their plans for the future, and all in fact do this, some attempting to match these against internal pots or funds that have particular maturity and liquidity profiles. The latter can, and do, carry out macroeconomic modelling. If, for example, a country is oil-rich, then the amount of proven reserves and the speed with which they are being used will suggest the time at which the fund will need to become a net payer rather than a net recipient of money. Rather vague, perhaps, but as the time to assumed zero oil grows shorter, then the forecasts will become increasingly less uncertain.

Do money purchase schemes have 'liabilities'?

Finally, what about money purchase (defined contribution – DC) pension funds? The trustees, consultants and sponsors of such schemes appear largely to take the view that they have no liabilities at all, since the investment risk has been transferred to each individual member, who will receive on retirement whatever pot has been accumulated, be it large or small, with which to buy an annuity. It is submitted that such a view, though doubtless correct in law (at least at the time of writing) is hardly an ethical one.

In many cases, those who now hold a money purchase pension scheme previously held, or had been led to expect to hold, a final salary one. What this means, in effect, did they but know it, is that they are now sitting on the expectation of a dramatically reduced level of benefits during retirement, perhaps as little as a third of what a healthy final salary scheme might have provided.[1]

Previously, the pension fund and its sponsor held both the risk of being able to pay the retirement benefits, and the risk of investing its assets, both of which might be articulated as the risk that at some time in the future the fund would not have enough capital to be able to pay the retirement benefits for which it was liable. With the closure of a final salary scheme and the substitution of a money purchase scheme, both of these risks are transferred to other people. Now the pension scheme member is forced (in the case of an average size pension pot) to buy an annuity from a provider such as a life insurance company, and the amount of this annuity will be a function partly of prevailing annuity rates (which are closely linked to government bond yields) and partly of the money value of the member's personal pot on retirement.

Thus the scheme no longer has the risk of payment, since this has been transferred to the annuity provider. Nor does it have the risk of investment, since it matters not a jot to the trustees how large or small any individual pot might be. That investment risk has now been transferred to the individual member. Yet, given that in most cases the member has very little say as to how that money should be invested within the scheme, and that many would argue that trustee incompetence played a large part in bringing about the funding crisis in the first place, this is a situation that to many may feel to be morally unpalatable.

Even a few years ago, an ethical discussion might have been felt to sit rather oddly in a book on investment strategy but, as we have already seen when considering possible internal limitations on freedom of choice such as SRI, there is now a general acceptance that the two cannot and should not be divorced. It would, one hopes, now be difficult for the trustees of any pension scheme that has made this transition (which, remember, represents a massive admission of failure by the trustees concerned in their own custody of the pension scheme to date) not to be forced to show that they have at least had this discussion.

What they decide will be a matter for their own consciences, but it is surely arguable that their objective should be to assure that the annuity which each member receives on retirement should match as closely

---

1. Guy Fraser-Sampson, *No Fear Finance*, London: Kogan Page, 2011.

as possible the level of benefits they might previously have expected under a final salary scheme. At the very least, they should surely offer members the option of various investment and contribution combinations, at least some of which might come somewhere close to fulfilling this goal.

Lest this be thought fanciful, it should be pointed out that in some countries more enlightened than the UK, the closure of a final salary scheme is not permitted except on condition that the sponsor first makes supplemental payments into it based on exactly such a calculation. It is therefore the misfortune of any member of a British occupational pension scheme to be living in a country where public policy often seems to reinforce and encourage unethical behaviour rather than the reverse.

Incidentally, a number of DC pensions schemes have, albeit somewhat belatedly, begun to recognise that both investment returns and time horizons do matter after all, and a section later in the chapter describes these developments.

The importance of the investment time horizon

As we have seen, we can use a model of our future liabilities to calculate our target rate of investment return, flexing the model as necessary for uncertainty of future outcomes, and deciding what approach to adopt to inflation. So we have now calculated the 'What' that we wish to achieve. This may seem a very fundamental, even a simplistic, thing to be describing, but the awful truth is that most institutional investors never even get this far. This is doubly unfortunate, for not only will they have no idea of what their target rate of return might be, but also they will have no clear idea of the extent to which they are long- or short-term investors, which in turn means they will have little idea as to how to approach their task.

Having delineated the 'What' we must now turn to the 'When'. As Napoleon said, where you march to is only part of the story; the timing is also important. If you get to the battlefield a day early you may well guarantee success through being able to prepare your positions in advance, but if you get there a day too late, your side will already have been defeated. Again, though, this point is routinely ignored by investors.

It seems so obvious and so instinctively a commonsense proposition that the time scale of our investments should match that of our liabilities that we need to explore in some detail the reasons why this does not actually happen in practice.

We shall look at this shortly, but first, in order to forestall the clamouring of pension consultants claiming that this is what they already do, let us be clear what we are talking about. Pension funds do indeed try to match the duration (which is a slightly different, and rather technical measure[2]) of their bond holdings to the duration of their liabilities. However, this process is fundamentally flawed.

First, and most obviously, it simply is not possible, at least not at present. There simply are not enough long-term government bonds available (nor indeed long-enough government bonds, which is not as pedantic a distinction as it appears), particularly in the USA, where the duration of public debt is much shorter than in the UK. Thus there will always in practice be a gap between the two.

Second, it makes a number of assumptions, none of which can be sustained. It assumes that bonds are the only instruments a pension fund needs within its portfolio. It also assumes that the liabilities will not change, which in turn assumes that the affect of neither inflation nor longevity upon those liabilities will change. As we have already seen, attempting to protect a portfolio against these forces may sometimes be possible, but only to some extent, and usually only at a significant extra cost. It also assumes that the pension fund is already at least fully funded on an actuarial basis.

It is therefore difficult to avoid the conclusion that pension consultants none the less persist in the idea of matching the duration of bonds and liabilities simply because it saves them from having to indulge in any real thinking. It also saves them from having to learn about any exotic asset types (for 'exotic' read 'anything other than bonds') apart from perhaps equities, where at least they can take refuge in the comforting illusion of volatility-as-risk. Conveniently for them, it is also an approach that has become widely enshrined in legislation and regulation.

Problems with time (1): the tyranny of periodic returns

The first problem we encounter is in fact a direct consequence of the great volatility confidence trick. Even those who spend hours every day finding standard deviations rarely stop to think about how they are calculated, or why.

Standard deviation is a measure of volatility. It is derived from something called variance.[3] Variance in turn is a measure of the distance away from the average (mean) that the 'observations' (the individual data points) within a sample occur. Thus a sample showing a low variance and standard deviation will be tightly clustered around the average, whereas one with high variance and standard deviation will be widely scattered with some individual data points occurring a large distance above or below the average.

---

2. Explained in Guy Fraser-Sampson, *No Fear Finance*, pp. 145–50.
3. Standard deviation is the square root of variance.

What are these data points? They are the periodic investment returns of whatever asset, or asset type, is being considered. The period in question will depend on the type of analysis being conducted. At one extreme, annual returns are often considered to be sufficient for asset allocation purposes, whereas with Value at Risk (VaR) exercises daily returns are used. VaR measures the biggest loss that a particular portfolio is likely to suffer in one day, and thus the use of daily returns is entirely appropriate. What is less clear is whether VaR actually tells an investor anything remotely useful for them to know.

So, periodic returns may be annual, quarterly, monthly, weekly or daily. The important thing to remember is what they measure: the return of an asset or asset type *within a particular period*. This is a vitally important point.

Problems with time (2): inappropriate benchmarking

This preoccupation with periodic returns blinds investors to the fact that there is another type of return measure far more closely aligned to the business of long-term investing, namely techniques such as an IRR, which measure the return of an investment *over a number of periods*. Not only is it a better fit from a time point of view, it also has two other very important advantages.

First, it is a cash measure. It works by observing when real cash flows actually occur and then calculating the return they produce. Periodic returns do not do this. They operate on a 'mark to market' basis. If you buy some Coca-Cola shares in March and by December their market price has declined 10 per cent you will be recorded as having suffered a 10 per cent loss, but of course you haven't. You would have made a loss if you had sold the shares, but you may not be intending to sell them for many years. So why should you be placed with a loss you have not actually incurred, a loss that is purely notional? What an IRR does is to look at the negative cash flow when you buy a share, then the positive cash flow that comes when you sell it, as well as any intervening positive cash flows from dividend payments, and then calculates the cash-on-cash return across the whole holding period.

If you adopt the periodic approach instead, then the 'value' of your asset will go merrily up and down each year, thus creating the volatility that allows you to measure the 'risk' of your investment, but actually its risk is something else entirely, as we shall see shortly. Yet each of these gains or losses is notional, not real. They are contingent gains and losses that only harden into reality when you finally sell the asset for cash. What should matter to an investor is the actual cash return they make over the precise period for which they hold the asset, not the notional gain or loss with which they are marked over the course of an arbitrary period such as a calendar year.

The second advantage is that an IRR, unlike a periodic measure, takes into account the time value of money. An IRR recognises that the further out into the future a cash flow occurs, the less value it has for you today. In fact, this is how an IRR is calculated, by finding the discount rate that will reduce the net present value of the relevant cash flows to zero. Don't worry if you don't understand this concept. What is important is that you grasp the fact that a cash flow that occurs in the future has less value to you than one of the same amount that occurs today. After all, would you rather have 10 dollars today, or 10 dollars in a year's time?

An IRR incorporates this understanding of the time value of money, whereas a periodic return does not. Instead, the return of an asset across time is 'annualised' by taking a simple average of the periodic returns that occurred during the holding period. Under this method, the value of each year's return is assumed to be constant, regardless of when it actually occurred. In other words, if you make a big gain in the tenth year of owning an asset, it is assumed to bring you the same benefit as making it straightaway in the first year.

Since compound returns have so many advantages over periodic returns, why are they not widely used? The answer involves a classic 'Catch-22' situation, and again the culprit is the myth of volatility-as-risk. Investors believe that volatility and risk are the same thing. Volatility can only be measured using periodic returns, therefore investors use periodic returns.

Problems with time (3): career risk

A direct consequence of the tyranny of periodic returns is that they focus attention on what happens within a single period, such as a calendar year, rather than over an investor's real time horizon which, as we have seen above, might be as long as several decades, depending on the time period over which future liabilities are modelled to arise. This is a disaster for those who are held responsible for the performance of a portfolio, and triggers a reaction which in fact makes poor performance much more likely.

It means that most investment managers are assessed on how they have performed over the course of a single year, being rewarded if they have achieved a high return, and punished, or even dismissed, if they have under-performed. Even so, there is another layer of illogicality, since the benchmark chosen is usually something arbitrary such as an equity index, or a specific number plucked out of the air, rather than a meaningful figure such as the investor's target rate of return.

It is now widely recognised that career risk, the justifiable fear of prejudicing one's employment prospects, plays a major role in all business decision-making. In the case of investment management, it has one predictable consequence. The two predominant desires a manager will feel will be (1) to match a given benchmark as closely as possible; and (2) to design a portfolio with as little potential downside as possible.

Recognising the importance of time horizons in DC pension fund investing

As mentioned above, there is a particular aspect of investing the assets of DC pension plans that deserves a special mention, namely the technique of matching the chosen assets with the different time horizons of different members. This has been around for some years as a general theory (usually labelled, rather confusingly, 'lifestyle' investing) but has more recently been seen as a specialist and complex area, perhaps so that those who advise pension funds can justify charging high fees for their advice and for creating appropriate fund products. In truth, though, both the theory and the required execution are simple and could easily be accomplished for themselves by any individual investor with a self-administered pension plan.

The crucial element that is required in being able to envisage such an approach is also what is required to break the intellectual log-jam that prevents intelligent investment of pension fund assets around the world. It is the need to recognise that the traditional blinkered mind-set of 'volatility bad, liquidity good', discussed in Chapter 5 is mistaken, at least in so far as it applies to longer-term investors. To illustrate this point, let us consider two different DC pension fund members.

Susan is 63 years old and planning to retire in about three years' time. She has been a member of the pension fund for over 30 years and has accumulated a reasonable, though not large, pension pot. She will be required to use most of this to buy an annuity when she retires.

Stephen is 30 years old and is planning to work until he is at least 65. He has thus far accumulated little by way of a pension pot but is fairly relaxed about this, as both he and his employer will be making contributions into the fund for the next 35 years.

Both Susan and Stephen have one thing in common, and one thing only (other than their membership of the same pension scheme). They will both be required to buy an annuity when they retire and will be required to use all or most of the accrued value of their pension pot to purchase it. Their time horizons, though, are totally different, and this has some important implications. It means that Susan is essentially a short-term investor, while Stephen is a long-term one.

For Susan, it would be a major disaster were the value of her pension pot to decline significantly over the next three years, since it would leave her with a lower annuity to fund her retirement than she would otherwise have received. Stephen, on the other hand, should be largely indifferent of such a decline. While, of course, he would much prefer that it goes up in value rather than down, if he is a rational investor he will acknowledge that it is what happens over the course of the next 30 years that matters, not the next three. Further, if one believes that if one accepts a higher level of risk, then one can also justifiably expect higher returns, at least over the long term, then for a long-term investor such as Stephen, volatility is actually a good thing, a desirable thing and not, as Markowitz said in his landmark 1952 paper,[4] an undesirable thing.

Similarly with liquidity. Susan needs to be in a position to purchase her annuity in three years' time, and in order to so this she needs cash, which in turn means she needs to be holding assets that can easily and quickly be turned into cash. It is no good her holding things such as interests in private equity or infrastructure funds for which no public market exists, and which will generate cash only sporadically and perhaps unpredictably over many years. She needs to have assets such as prime government bonds in her portfolio, which can be sold easily for cash even in abnormal market conditions.

Stephen, on the other hand, should normally be looking to have as little liquidity in his portfolio as possible, perhaps even none at all. For, as David Swensen, veteran CIO of the Yale Endowment, points out, liquidity comes at a heavy price in the shape of lower expected long-term returns.[5] For Stephen to hold unnecessary liquidity, such as government bonds, would be like trying to drive his car with the handbrake on. They can only ever act as a drag on investment returns. For Susan, this is a price worth paying. For Stephen, it is not.

Tragically, many British pension funds have ignored this principle and continued to invest on behalf of DC ('money purchase') scheme members in much the same way as if they were assured of final salary protection, though thankfully this mind-set is gradually changing, driven not just by the switch to DC provision but also by auto-enrolment. The People's Pension, for example, offers an 'adventurous' option, but even this only comprises quoted equities, thus shunning illiquid assets entirely.

In other parts of the world, lifestyle investing and 'target date' funds are increasingly becoming part of the landscape. The latter, as pointed out above, seem simply to be complicated and expensive versions offered by

---

4. Harry Markowitz, 'Portfolio Selection', *Journal of Finance,* vol. 7, no. 1, 1952.

5. David Swensen, *Pioneering Portfolio Management* (2nd edn), New York: Pocket Books, 2009.

third parties of something that pension trustees, or even their members, could and should be doing for themselves using exchange-traded funds (ETFs). The idea is exactly as suggested above, with younger members holding mainly illiquid and volatile assets, and transitioning over time to a purely bond-like portfolio as they approach retirement age. The rate at which this transition happens is called the 'glide path' and is naturally the subject of much learned debate and expensive advice.

How can we pull all this together?

So, as we have seen, if we are a long-term investor, or for that part of our portfolio in respect of which we are a long-term investor, we should be working towards a situation in which we can summarise our investment objectives with reference to two parameters: (1) long-term compound return; and (2) liability (and thus also investment) time horizon. The former should be a calculated (or at least assessed) number based on probable liabilities, while the latter is based on the period over which you choose to model your liabilities.

This is in marked contrast to current practice, whereby investors, in so far as they state these things at all, use (1) an 'annualised' (average annual) return; and (2) volatility (some number of standard deviations) but all subject to some sort of umbrella level of liquidity. In practice these numbers will also be chosen arbitrarily in a vacuum, and not calculated.

This in turn has very significant implications for how we choose to go about implementing our investment process. If you set off on a journey without knowing where you are going or how long you have to allow to get there, it is hardly surprising if you choose the wrong route, the wrong mode of transport, or even get lost completely. Yet the sad truth is that this is exactly what most investors around the world end up doing.

In the coming chapters we shall examine a more intelligent way of proceeding. In particular, we need to ensure that there is a steady and logical progression from one stage of the process to the next. So, having considered what sort of investor we are, what we are trying to achieve, what resources we have available to us with which to try to do so, and to what limitations our freedom of action might be subject, we now need to turn to considering the sorts of assets in which we should be investing and (an important point and often overlooked) how.

7
Asset Allocation: Theory and Practice

The question 'What sorts of assets should we invest in?' may seem a very fundamental one, and indeed it is. Yet not so fundamental that we should begin our journey with it, as most investors do. Having read this far you will appreciate that there are a lot of preliminary questions we have to ask first, not least 'What sorts of investor are we?' and 'What are we trying to achieve?'. Having done so, however, it does indeed mark a very significant stage in the journey, where we move from a largely inward-looking process, examining our own circumstances, to an outward-looking one considering various types of asset and methods of investment.

In doing this we are faced with yet another of those paradoxes that seem to characterise finance and investment. The choice of available assets in which to invest has never been wider, particularly in the case of retail investors, who were traditionally very limited in their options, and yet in many cases the actual range of assets selected has never been narrower. At the extreme, we find many investors around the world who hold mainly or predominantly the bonds of their own domestic government, and others who grudgingly add some other types of fixed income assets as well as a few quoted equities.

We have already touched on many of the reasons for this. By far the most powerful is the determination of governments and the central banks whom they control (whether overtly or covertly) to create and maintain a false market in their own securities. This can be done openly through bond-purchasing exercises in the secondary market, such as quantitative easing (QE), or, less obviously, by regulations that force domestic financial institutions to hold government bonds, or at least strongly discourage them from doing otherwise.

Rational investors would, of course, refuse to participate in a false market, hence the need for regulation effectively to force them to do so whether they like it or not. The use of international and/or supra-national measures such as Basel III and Solvency II reinforce this coercion by creating a sort of market manipulation support group for finance ministers and central bankers, operated by financial regulators.

The consequences, both direct and indirect, spread far beyond the area initially affected. Directly, there is a knock-on effect on fixed income instruments of all descriptions, whatever their term (time period), denomination, or type of issuer (government or corporate). For the pricing (and thus the yield, since the two are inversely related) of all bond-type instruments is assessed with regard to that great standby of financial theory, the fabled risk-free rate of return. No matter how ridiculous this might seem, given the mass downgrading of government credit ratings around the world, this is still assumed to be the same thing as the short-term government bond rate. Thus, if the yield on government bonds is manipulated to an artificially low rate so that heavily indebted governments can carry on borrowing when the markets would not normally allow them to do so, so is the yield on corporate bonds also artificially depressed. You may still be applying an appropriate differential, but to too low a base rate.

Indirectly, this impacts disastrously on, for example, pension funds and their members in two specific ways, one obvious but the other less so. First, it means that pension funds make less income than they would otherwise do, and thus have less money available when the time comes to meet their liabilities. Indeed, at the time of writing, the real yields on government bonds in many countries, including the UK and the USA, are negative. In other words, by holding government bonds, pension funds are guaranteed to lose money once inflation has been taken into account. Hardly something that could be classified as an 'investment' at all, many would argue.

Second, in the case of DC (money purchase) pension fund members, who form an increasing majority of those who are approaching retirement age, they are required (unless they have an unusually large pension pot) to purchase an annuity to provide them with an annual income in retirement. What is not generally understood is that annuity rates are in turn based on bond yields. Thus, for any given capital sum, pensioners will receive a much lower amount of income than they would otherwise have done. So, whoever QE might have benefited (and it seems highly doubtful that it has actually benefited anyone at all apart from governments[1]) it has been poison to pensioners and pension funds.

---

1. Certainly in the UK it failed dismally in its originally stated intention of boosting lending. In fact, M4 lending *fell* steadily after its introduction.

Of course, there are also other reasons. Chiefly, there is the fetish of liquidity, which many cite as the reason for not looking beyond bonds and quoted equities. We have already noted the illogicality of this in an earlier chapter. Liquidity comes at a heavy price in the shape of lower expected long-term returns, and so investors should actually hold as little of these kinds of holdings as possible, rather than as much as possible. Yet even ignoring this, investors' actions still do not stand up to scrutiny.

After all, if one is seeking liquidity, then what about active currency (which is cash) or gold, which is not only as liquid as money itself (as noted earlier, gold is often referred to as a currency without a country) but holds its value even if money ceases to have any? What about commodities and energy assets, all of which can be instantly traded on recognised global markets? All are liquid, yet all are ignored. The sad truth is that the fetish of liquidity is simply a device which the timid, the stubborn and the uninformed can and do use as an excuse not to have to put in the hard work and independent thinking required to look at other asset types.

Yet there is further illogicality at work here as well. As we saw in Chapter 4, there is widespread misunderstanding as to the nature of investment risk, with most of the world's investors choosing to equate it with the volatility (variance) of historic periodic returns. Again, this is the refuge of the intellectually sloppy, who do not wish to have to exercise independent thought or venture into any difficult territory. It is the classic 'liquidity good, volatility bad' mantra, which many chant whenever they are asked their opinion on any investment idea.

Yet it contains another obvious paradox. Liquid assets go up and down in value (assuming value and price to be the same thing) every minute, even every second, since that is the way that quoted markets work. Illiquid assets are usually based not on market price but on underlying asset values, which tend to remain relatively constant over time, albeit subject to regular professional revaluation. Therefore, assuming you are marking your assets to market, which financial regulation universally requires you to do, you cannot have more liquidity in your portfolio without also having more volatility. Gold, for example, is perhaps the most liquid asset there is, but can also be highly volatile in the short term. 'Liquidity good, volatility bad' is a nonsense – you cannot increase the former without also increasing the latter. Even government bond prices are volatile if you measure them relative to themselves over time (rather than relative to equity prices, as some sneaky consultants do).

We shall look in a moment at the sorts of assets investors now have available from which to choose, but let us first think about why it might make sense to move beyond bonds and equities into what are still disparagingly called 'alternative' assets. Incidentally, as we do so, let us remind ourselves once more that we are considering investors here who are either long-term in their entirety (such as a sovereign wealth fund) or have a part of their liabilities, and thus also their portfolio, that is long-term in nature. All pension funds, for example, would fall into this latter category.

We have already looked at one very strong argument in favour of certain alternative assets; those that are illiquid, such as private equity, real estate, infrastructure, agricultural and timber assets; and (in practice) many hedge funds. Here, a rational investor should be looking to make use of the illiquidity premium, the principle that we give up short-term liquidity in exchange for the expectation of higher long-term returns. Indeed, if we follow this argument to its logical but absurd conclusion, a rational investor would hold *only* illiquid assets.

Logical because a rational investor should seek out the highest possible return; but absurd because investment return is often not the only criterion – regulatory issues, for example, will rear their heads for many investors. Absurd too because, for reasons we will shortly explore, it may not be possible to find enough illiquid asset classes in which to invest. For example, these 'private market' asset types will in many cases be subject to issues of access and selection that may render them impractical for some investors, particularly those with very small amounts of assets under management.

As we saw earlier in this chapter, it is a great mistake to assume, as many investors seem to do, that alternative assets must necessarily be illiquid. Some, such as gold and active currency, are even more liquid than bonds and equities, while others, such as commodity and energy assets, are arguably no less so. This supposed illiquidity is yet another myth about alternative assets being peddled by those who for whatever reason do not want to have to consider them.

Those who are interested in learning about these various assets in more detail may wish to refer to a recent work of mine.[2] In roughly descending order of liquidity they include gold and other precious metals; active currency; industrial metals; oil and gas; agricultural commodities; hedge funds (a phrase which covers an enormous range of investment techniques); real estate (property); private equity; infrastructure; agricultural land; and timber plantations. In addition there are the so-called 'exotics' into which many investors are increasingly being tempted; these include diamonds, art, antiques, coins and stamps.

---

2. Guy Fraser-Sampson, *Alternative Assets: Investments for a Post-Crisis World*, Chichester, UK: John Wiley, 2011.

The required attitude towards all these different asset types can be summed up very briefly. With the exception only of the exotics, they are equally valid and as worthwhile as traditional mainstream bond and equity assets. There may well be practical or financial reasons for excluding some from our portfolio, but once something *has* been selected then there is no reason in principle why we should have more or less of it than anything else. It follows, as we shall see below, that if you are not prepared for whatever reason to make a significant allocation to a particular asset type, you would do far better not to consider it at all. This is yet another basic principle that is widely ignored in practice.

Three different approaches to asset allocation

Let us suppose that one of your friends has an accident at work and is badly injured: so badly injured in fact that they will never be able to work again. They do, however, receive a large compensation payment, and they come to you for advice on what they should do with it. There are probably three broad approaches you might suggest.

Option 1 would be to say 'Well, this is all the money you have to last you for the rest of your life, so the one thing you can't afford to do is to lose any of it.' If you were to pursue this approach, you would probably advise your friend to put everything in government bonds. The problem with Option 1, though, is inflation. Even if you are a tax-exempt investor there is no guarantee that bond yields will keep pace with inflation (as we have already noted, at the time of writing, bond yields in the UK are negative in real terms), while if you are a taxpayer the only guarantee is that bonds can never, ever, keep pace with inflation. So your friend is going to see the real value of their compensation payment steadily drain away year after year. If they are currently quite young, this is very bad news indeed. By the time they reach retirement age they will probably already be destitute.

Option 2 would be to say 'Well, you need to be able to add to the value of your portfolio, so you need to invest on the stock market.' There are various problems with this approach too. First, stock market returns tend to be heavily cyclical, and if they happen to be at the top of a cycle when your friend invests they may have to wait a long time just to get their starting capital back, even in nominal terms, much less after inflation. Second, people are beginning to realise that the period of strongly positive (at least at times) equity returns experienced since the 1990s may actually be an aberration, an exception rather than the rule. Certainly, if you look at equity returns in 20-year chunks, historical returns have often struggled even to match inflation. So the idea that just putting all your money on the stock market is some sort of free ride to riches, even in the long term, is starting to appear a rather dangerous one.

Most of the world's investors choose to implement some combination of Option 1 ('Don't invest at all') and Option 2 ('Let's put everything in equities and see what happens'), hoping presumably that they will receive the best, rather than the worst, of both worlds. There is, however, another way.

Option 3 might be to say 'Here are five small buckets. Why don't you put 20 per cent of your money into each of these buckets? By the way, I have chosen them in such a way that, at least if historical returns are any sort of guide at all, they should not all go up and down at the same time as each other.' What has just been described is pretty much what has come to be known as the Yale Model, as practised by David Swensen, whom we have already met.

Yes, of course, this approach is subject to the reservation that we are assuming we may use the past to predict the future, but no more so than the other two options, and in fact probably rather less so. For here we are not so much concerned with the actual level of returns, nor even with whether they are likely to go out of their predicted range, but only with their general pattern relative to each other, which is what we call correlation.

Correlation

Let us first understand exactly what correlation is or, more correctly, what it represents or measures, and then consider its strengths and weaknesses when used as an aid to investment decision-making.

Correlation is sometimes confused with volatility, which is perhaps understandable since neither of them are concepts most of us meet in everyday life. The easiest way to remember the difference between them is that volatility measures the extent to which *one* thing (in this case an investment price or return, depending on which is being measured) moves up and down over time, whereas correlation measures the extent to which *two* such things move up and down together at the same time.

Imagine two stocks that were locked together in some way and thus always moved in the same way. If one went up 5 per cent one day then the other one would also go up 5 per cent on the same day (similarly, they would both go down together). We would say that these two assets were perfectly correlated. If we were to measure the correlation of their respective market prices over time (which we can do using the Excel function =CORREL)[3] then we would find that it was 100 per cent.

Equally, if we had two shares where one was the mirror image of the other, going down 5 per cent every time the other went up 5 per cent, we would have perfect negative correlation, and were we to repeat our calculation the answer this time would be −100 per cent.

Naturally it is all-but impossible to find examples of perfect correlation in practice, whether negative or positive. Even bonds issued by the same government are not perfectly correlated, since they will each have a different lifetime length ('term'), and long-term bonds are generally slightly less expensive than short-term bonds to enable the investor to be offered a slightly higher return as a reward for being prepared to buy uncertainty for a longer time.

So, when we talk of assets being 'highly-correlated' or 'lowly-correlated' or even 'uncorrelated' with each other we are talking about matters of degree. Two good examples can be given, one each of high and low correlation. The Financial Times and Stock Exchange (FTSE) and Standard & Poor's (S&P) quoted indices are highly correlated with each other, and even when total return is used (adding in the dividend yield) remain high, though less so since British companies have traditionally paid higher dividends. Natural gas and crude oil prices, on the other hand, have, perhaps surprisingly, shown negative correlation with each other.

Incidentally, the first of these two cases demonstrates an important principle. Many investors in search of diversification have sought to buy something 'different' to put in their portfolios, and many UK investors have in fact 'diversified' into US quoted equities. Yet, as our example shows, they did not buy themselves any real diversification at all. For diversification is not about buying something 'different', but something which may *behave* differently within your portfolio. It follows from this that it also matters not at all what an asset is called or how it is classified, yet another vital lesson which could usefully be learnt by most of the world's investors. The label you have chosen to put on the box is irrelevant – all that matters is how the contents of the box are likely to behave within your own individual portfolio.

Correlation is, rightly, being recognised increasingly as a possible missing magic ingredient in the investment mix. It is not the function of this book to teach basic finance theory, but any investors who are not already familiar with the concept of extending the efficient frontier (see

---

3. First enter the two price series on separate lines of the spreadsheet then enter '=CORREL(range1,range2)', where range1 and range2 are the two series cut and pasted from their respective lines.

below) should become so without delay, since it lies at the heart of modern investment strategy.[4]

Briefly, it must logically be correct that, for any given level of 'risk' (volatility) one can construct a notional portfolio which gives the highest possible level of return for the specified level of risk. This is not to suggest that anybody actually does this. After all, to do so you would need to be in the future, looking backwards to today. Those of us without the benefit of a time machine have no idea how any given investments are likely to perform in the future. But, clearly, if one could construct an infinite number of notional portfolios all showing the same volatility but with different mixes of assets within them, then one of them would over time earn a higher return than any of the others. This would be known as the efficient portfolio, or the optimal portfolio, and it sits on a line known as the efficient frontier, which is drawn by plotting the relationship between the risk and return of every efficient portfolio – one for each value of risk.

By adding lowly-correlated assets to our efficient portfolio it is possible in certain cases to move it beyond this line, something that traditional finance theory would hold to be impossible, since it posits a fixed relationship between 'risk' (volatility) and return, just as Newton's universe envisaged a fixed relationship between space and time. For example, by mixing together judiciously the past prices of natural gas and crude oil within a portfolio you can both increase its average annual return and decrease its volatility.

With belated enlightenment has often come undue enthusiasm. The search for 'uncorrelated returns' has in many quarters assumed the proportions of the quest for the Holy Grail. This is to be welcomed, since it lifts discussion of asset allocation to a much more sophisticated plane, but with caution, since many have allowed their excitement with this magical substance to blind them to possible drawbacks and objections, since while it can undeniably be effective in boosting overall returns, there are a number of theoretical reservations of which one needs to be aware, if only to defend a correlation-based approach from its critics (of whom there are many).

Some drawbacks to the use of correlation

The first objection is that the output of your correlation calculations will vary, depending both on what period of returns you take for comparison, and on how frequently you sample within a given period.

---

4. See, for example, *No Fear Finance* (cited in Chapter 6), where it is explained in both text and graphically.

The first limb of this poses particular practical problems, because different return bases began at different times. For example, in the illustration just given of natural gas and crude oil, the price data for gas begins well after the price data for oil; and the FTSE 100 index of UK blue chip stocks began well after the S&P index in America. So, yes, the period you choose to study will affect the correlation figure.

The second limb impacts particularly on differences of approach when practising something like VaR as opposed to strategic asset allocation, even if you are looking at the same timespan of returns. If you look at the same 20 years, for example, VaR practitioners will be calculating daily correlation while their investment strategy colleagues will usually be using annual correlation.

These things are all perfectly true, but are generally ignored for investment strategy purposes. After all, correlation is only one dial on the dashboard, and others, such as volatility, return, liquidity and inflation will also be used in any decision-making. Incidentally, exactly the same objections hold true in respect of calculating volatility, but none of the traditional Newtonian persuasion seem to worry too much about this.

The second objection is that correlation can change over time, and sometimes quite dramatically, as seemed to happen in and around 2008. It is all very well, the critics say, calculating that something has exhibited 40 per cent correlation with quoted equities over the last 20 years, but if it suddenly goes to 75 per cent within the course of a single year, then how meaningful is the original calculation? There are two points to consider here.

The first is, though there is no way of proving this mathematically from available data, it seems as though at least a large part of the sudden surge in correlation around 2008 was man-made. As was pointed out earlier, investment is at least as much about emotion as it is about reason, and there are times when it becomes heavily driven by emotion. When panic takes over people may well all start selling similar things at the same time, which is pretty much what happened in 2008, particularly in areas such as hedge funds. This was exacerbated by people realising that they had misjudged the liquidity of various assets (such as corporate bonds) in extreme market conditions (such as the collapse of Lehman Brothers). Yet a long-term investor should never *have* to sell anything. On the contrary, they can treat market downturns as buying opportunities. The problem is that this requires enormous personal courage: to be holding, or even buying, when everyone else is selling.

The second point is that this is only really a problem if you believe that in finance (1) we can use the past to predict the future; and (2) that normal distribution always applies to investment returns (the second being in practice a sub-set of the first). Sadly, many investors do actually believe this, but let it be stated for the record that neither of these assumptions holds true. Investment is an art, not a science. Past data may provide useful guidelines, principles, and even hypotheses, but that is all they are. They are simply a number of different dials on the dashboard which an experienced investor will use to form a judgement about what to do next. Unfortunately, many investors seem to believe that finance is a science and that its rules are absolute, objective and predictive. They are not. In fact, they are probably not even 'rules' at all in any scientific sense.

The gravest objection of all is yet to come, though ironically it is the one that its critics fail to identify, since they do not understand even why it is a problem at all.

Like volatility, correlation can only be measured using *periodic* returns. It does not matter what sort of period you take, be it annual, quarterly, monthly, weekly or even daily. The calculation only works if you can plug in two time series of data, and any time series data must necessarily be periodic in nature.

Yet, as we saw when we examined volatility, there are two important objections to the unthinking adoption of periodic returns when looking at investment performance. The first is that, for the reasons stated in Chapter 6, they arguably do not properly represent the reality to an investor of holding an actual investment in real life. The second is that there are various asset types for which periodic returns are, for various practical reasons, not a valid return measure.

These are all assets that might be described as 'cash-flow type assets', and while finance theory is happy to apply a different approach to the ones they like (bonds, which are measured using compound returns) they illogically deny it to the others, which include private equity, infrastructure and real estate as well as various energy type assets such as oil and gas royalties. Thus, we should be careful about 'correlation' figures for these asset types because they can only be calculated using heavily contrived annual returns, which in many cases give a misleading view of actual performance.

The Yale Model

So, now that we understand both the pros and cons of using correlation as part of our investment thinking, we can turn again to our Option 3, five-bucket approach, which is pretty much encapsulated, at least in broad principle, by the Yale Model.

David Swensen's book[5] offers a revealing insight into his thinking. We have already encountered his thoughts on liquidity, but let us take a look

---

5. *Pioneering Portfolio Management* (2nd edn) (cited in Chapter 6).

at another important feature of his work which sets Yale and some of its fellow US college endowments apart from most of the rest of the world's investors.

Swensen is generally credited with having pioneered the approach of using several roughly equal buckets of assets. The idea is that, as well as being so far as possible illiquid, and thus likely to generate higher long-term returns, they should be as far as possible uncorrelated. This latter requirement is, of course, subject to the reservations recorded above.

An important point, which follows from this principle, is that no allocation should be made to any individual asset type unless it is substantial. Swensen was originally talking about any allocation of less than about 15 per cent being difficult to justify. I always felt that this was perhaps setting the bar too high, particularly for very large investors such as sovereign wealth funds, who might find it difficult to deploy 15 per cent of their total assets in any one area without being pushed down the manager quality scale.[6] So 10 per cent may be preferred for large investors, but the general principle holds true. For anyone other than a very large investor, 15 per cent remains a good guideline, and 20 per cent probably even more so. A failure to recognise and observe this principle is one of the most common mistakes made by investors and consultants around the world. It is not infrequent to see asset type allocations as ridiculously low as 3 per cent. Such investors would do far better not to be allocating to the asset type at all.

There are two reasons for this, one obvious (though not so obvious that most investors completely ignore it) and the other less so.

The first is that unless you have a substantial part of your assets allocated to any particular area, then its performance can have no significant impact on the overall performance of your portfolio as a whole, so why do it?

The second is that if you make a very small allocation to something then you are most unlikely to be prepared to invest the time, budget and resources to it to pursue it in a proper, professional manner. If you make a 20 per cent allocation to infrastructure, for example, it is likely that your first move will be to call an international head-hunter to find you one of the world's leading experts on infrastructure investing to head up the initiative. If, on the other hand, you make a 3 per cent allocation to infrastructure you are likely instead to drag some hapless individual out of your fixed income team and bestow upon them the title of 'head of infrastructure investing', with predictable results.

So the rationale of the Yale Model is (1) to choose about five different asset 'buckets', each for a different asset type, and make roughly equal

---

allocations to each; (2) to avoid as far as possible liquid investments, since these are likely to under-perform in the long term; and (3) to choose asset 'buckets' that are as far as possible uncorrelated with each other so that one hopes you will never have a situation where all your asset types are producing negative returns at the same time.

This last principle might take a little explaining. After all, if you are constructing a portfolio in which you hope that not everything will ever be heading downwards at the same time, does it not also follow that not everything is likely to head *up* at the same time? If so, how is this rational, since surely you are deliberately aiming to cap your possible return?

The answer, as with so much in investment, is 'Yes, but…'. Yes, but there is actually some arithmetical justification for the well-known cognitive bias that investors are much more sensitive to losses than to gains. Not enough to justify it completely (otherwise it would not be a recognised cognitive bias at all), but some.

Try this experiment with people within your organisation or your college class. Tell them they are considering an investment that might go down in value by 20 per cent in any one year, and ask them what sort of expected gain they would require in order to justify making that investment. The rational answer is actually 25 per cent, because, if we assume a starting value of 100 to make the example easier:

$$100 \times 80\% = 80$$
$$80 \times 125\% = 100$$

A loss of 20 per cent drops our asset value to 80. It now requires a gain of 25 per cent to take it back to 100. Yet see how many of your sample group actually arrive at this answer. Usually most stipulate for 40 per cent or more.

It is clear, though, that if you are trying to grow the asset value of your portfolio over time, a loss can hurt you more than a corresponding gain can help you. Let us continue our example, but suppose that this time the asset value goes up first and then down.

$$100 \times 120\% = 120$$
$$120 \times 80\% \ = 96$$

So, again, the gain would have needed to be 25 per cent, taking the asset value to 125, for a subsequent 20 per cent drop to take it back to 100.

In other words, provided such a tactic is not carried to extremes, it is actually sensible to be prepared to accept one asset or so that does not perform as well in good years, or might even make a loss, in return for one or more that may perform less badly in poor years, even perhaps making a gain. Had you held physical gold in 2008, for example, you would have made a comfortable gain while all hell was breaking lose around you in other asset classes.

Having examined briefly the main principles that lie behind asset allocation, let us proceed to their more practical application.

8
Asset Allocation in Practice

The theoretical basis of diversifying across different asset classes is straightforward. It makes little sense to diversify away specific risk *within* any one asset class if we are not prepared also to diversify away systemic risk *across* asset classes.

We can have a beautifully diversified portfolio of quoted equities within which we can prove mathematically that we have reached the point (usually at around 30 individual companies or slightly fewer) where we can add another company to the mix without having any significant impact on the standard deviation of the whole. Yet if all we have in our investment portfolio is that collection of quoted equities then we still have 100 per cent exposure to the risk of the quoted equities market from which we have chosen to select. In the jargon, our portfolio will still be totally dependent on equity beta. 'Beta' in this context simply means equity market risk (systemic risk) – the way in which markets as a whole (usually measured by a relevant index) move up and down over time, as a result largely of investor sentiment.

Investing across asset types, then, whether one calls it multi-asset class investing or not, is not some arcane practice of which good, solid, down-to-earth investors should be justifiably suspicious. On the contrary, it represents basic common sense and it should be those who do *not* properly diversify who are called to account.

There are, of course, a number of reasons why investors choose to treat multi-asset class investing as a dangerous substance to be locked safely away in the poisons cupboard. First, as we have already seen, there are a number of intellectual barriers to overcome, such as entrenched attitudes to things like liquidity, volatility and the way in which returns are measured.

Second, there is the need to do some reading and listening in order to learn enough about these supposedly exotic asset classes in order to be able to make investment decisions with confidence. There is an obvious

Catch-22 here. By far the best way to learn about these asset types is to go to conferences, or invite managers in for discussions and absorb at first hand the pros and cons of each one. Yet most investors do exactly the opposite, keeping themselves in a hermetically sealed environment for fear of contamination. Incidentally, setting modesty aside, there is also at least one very competent book on the subject of alternative assets to which investors might refer.[1]

Third, and perhaps just as fundamentally, there is the problem of exactly how one should go about planning a multi-asset class portfolio, and this is exacerbated by two further features. First, the fact that very few investors actually undertake any proper investment strategy process, so that when they do turn their minds to constructing such a portfolio they are attempting to set asset allocation levels in a vacuum. Second, the fact that no single asset allocation mix will be exactly right for any two investors, since both will have target returns and time horizons that are different, even if only slightly.

This, in turn, means that consultants, such as those who advise pension funds, have to do something in return for their fees as well as to give specific advice in terms that can be clearly understood and acted on by their clients, none of which they find appealing. They would much rather propose a 'one size fits all' approach, under which the fact that they are simply copying what other people are doing is seen as a justification for their actions, rather than (as logic would suggest) a cause for concern.

So, since there seems to be great concern that allocating across multiple asset types is in some way difficult or dangerous, let us turn our attention to the required process. Before we do so, let it be stressed once again, notwithstanding the constant repetition, that we are concerned here with the activities of a long-term investor, or with that part of an investor's portfolio being mentally set aside to cover long-term liabilities. Remember that we are defining a 'long-term' investor as someone who, whether in whole or in part, has some liabilities that will occur more than two or three years into the future and/or that are at least to some extent predictable both as to their timing and amount (subject to an appropriate uncertainty factor within the modelling process).

Constructing our palette

Before an artist begins work on an oil painting, they will prepare a palette of the colours they think they are likely to need to mix together to

---

1. Guy Fraser-Sampson, *Alternative Assets* (cited in Chapter 7).

create whatever effect they have in mind. Clearly, the composition of the palette will to a large extent be determined by the subject matter of the painting. A seascape will involve a lot of blues, whereas a summer land-scape is likely to require a lot of greens. It can be very useful to begin the asset allocation process in the same way.

First, we select every asset we can think of and find a good source of return data to tap into. This may sound simple, but is actually much more problematic than you might think, because we are dealing with asset types as a whole, and what we are looking for is some measure of market return – the 'beta' of that particular asset type. We shall be discussing this issue in more detail when we talk about passive and active investing, but for the moment let us simply note a few points and move on.

Returns

First, not all asset types have a beta in the true sense at all, while others may, but lack a reliable way of measuring it. Private equity funds would be a good example of the former, and real estate of the latter, with hedge funds somewhere in between. Don't worry if this seems a somewhat cur-sory explanation. We shall be dealing with this very important point in much more detail in a subsequent chapter.

Second, we have to consider what type of return is being measured in each case, and whether this methodology is being used consistently across all our chosen asset types. This can be a particular problem with quoted equity returns, for example. Are you looking simply at the index, which takes into account notional capital gains and losses but not income; or some sort of total return that takes dividends into account? And even then, are you assuming reinvestment of dividends or just receiving them as one-off cash flows? Whichever it is, you need to be sure that you are comparing apples with apples. For example, if you are comparing some sort of total return quoted equities measure with real estate, you need to be sure that, in respect of the latter, you are taking rental yield into account as well as property values.

Then, as we have already seen, some asset types do not really lend themselves to annual returns at all, good examples being private equity and infrastructure. Clearly, compromises have to be made here in order to reach some kind of working arrangement with colleagues who may be less knowledgeable about alternative assets.

In fact, a very amusing situation can arise. On being told, for exam-ple, that annual returns are of limited use for private equity funds, people none the less insist that they are used (they are available, for what it's worth, from industry data providers), only to find that on a

Sharpe ratio (volatility adjusted) basis they look extremely attractive and a much 'lower risk' than quoted equities. Faced with this apparent anomaly, they either refuse to consider private equity at all, on the grounds that 'something is clearly wrong with the figures', or, citing the same reason, simply change the figures to represent their own perceptions and prejudices.

It can, of course, be argued strongly that the only returns that really matter to a long-term investor are compound returns, since these (1) are calculated on actual cash flows; and (2) take into account the time value of money. So something like an IRR calculation should also feature on your palette, but be warned that it will be necessary to make some assumptions about the timing of purchase and sale, and the length of the holding period in between. Again, the key here is consistency. Make sure that you adopt the same time period for each asset type, and play around with some different assumptions along the way.

Standard deviation and the Sharpe ratio

No matter how much we may disagree with the 'volatility as risk' myth, we must none the less accept that (1) most investors do not; and (2) historic volatility is undeniably a useful dial to have on our dashboard, so having selected our time series of returns data and worked out the average, we can now calculate the standard deviation of those returns.

We can in turn use this to calculate the Sharpe ratio. This is a classic and simple formula, but despite being both widely used and straightforward it is still often calculated wrongly. Its fundamental purpose is to divide the average of a time series of return data by its standard deviation, thus:

$$\frac{average\ return}{standard\ deviation\ of\ return}$$

though there are some common algebraic symbols for this, using r for return and the Greek letter sigma (σ) for standard deviation, thus:

$$\frac{r}{\sigma r}$$

Many investors thus blithely go ahead and make this calculation. However, this is not correct. The Sharpe ratio applies not to the total return generated, but only to the *excess* return, which is defined as the difference between the actual return achieved and the risk-free rate that could have been achieved over the same period. Despite widespread downgrades of government credit ratings, the short-term bond rate is still adopted as the measure of the risk-free return, perhaps largely because everybody is still so emotionally attached to the Sharpe ratio that nobody wants to acknowledge that its most basic requirement, the risk-free return, almost certainly no longer exists, if indeed it ever did.

So, in addition to the return that has actually been earned by whatever asset type we are considering, we also need to track whatever we are taking as our risk-free return and deduct the latter from the former for each time unit (which will be each calendar year if using annual returns) to arrive at the excess return produced by our asset type, and we then need to perform the same average and standard deviation calculations on that series of data as we did with the total return. If we put the former over the latter, that will give us our Sharpe ratio output, thus:

$$\frac{ra - rf}{\sigma\,(ra - rf)}$$

where *ra* is the return generated by the asset type, and *rf* the risk-free rate of return, so that *ra* minus *rf* equals the excess return of the asset type.

Just because the Sharpe ratio may no longer be intellectually pure does not mean that it is not a valuable indicator. On the contrary, it is. The important thing to remember, though, is that it is simply one indicator out of several rather than, as many investors treat it, the one right answer that will drive your decision-making. For one thing, all it really measures is relative volatility, and having read this far you will know that, for some investors, volatility is either largely irrelevant or actually an attractive feature to be sought out.

Treat it properly, though, as just one dial on the dashboard, view it in combination with other factors and it becomes a valuable filtering mechanism. For example, if an asset type shows both a low average return and a low Sharpe ratio this should at the very least make us consider how it might justify a place in our portfolio.

As a rough rule of thumb, any investment scoring higher than 0.5 on the Sharpe ratio is well worth taking seriously, but the further one gets towards zero, or even dips below it, the more searching the questions that need to be asked.

Experienced investors will be aware that other measures are often also commonly used for analysis purposes, most notably the Treynor ratio, which looks at the excess return of a given portfolio relative to its beta, or systemic risk, but this has the disadvantage that it can only be applied to portfolios of similar securities and thus, while it can be used to rate, for example, long only equity managers it is useless for asset allocation purposes.

More useful, and something that can be used directly alongside the Sharpe ratio as an additional guideline, is the Sortino ratio. This is subject to the same limitation as the Sharpe ratio, namely that it is volatility based, but it has the important difference that it looks only at downside risk, whether absolute downside (less than zero) or, interestingly and usefully, relative downside (less than a pre-set target return). Unfortunately, it makes use of a more complex variance measure called semideviation, which cannot be calculated by means of a standard Excel function. However, Sortino ratio outputs can be calculated using specific financial plug-ins, or as part of specialist portfolio optimiser programs.

Please do not worry if you do not have the Sortino ratio available for use, or even do not understand fully what it does. It is mentioned above only for the sake of completeness, and from here onwards we shall consider only the Sharpe ratio.

Correlation

We now have the various elements of the traditional two-dimensional view of finance, albeit that we may have rather more, and more correctly calculated, than most investors are used to handling. However, as we know, this is only part of the story, and we now have to apply the third dimension of correlation.

It is suggested that the return analysis we have conducted so far is presented in vertical columns, the final lines of which will be average return, standard deviation and the Sharpe ratio score. Obviously, at the top of each column will be the name of the return measure we are examining.

Now let us take those descriptions and copy them vertically down the page below the Sharpe Ratio line. This will create a matrix on which we can plot the correlation of each asset type return with every other one. Suppose, for example, that one of our columns represents MSCI World. If we go down to where MSCI World now appears as the first cell in a horizontal line and work our way across one cell at a time, we can calculate the correlation of MSCI World with every other return measure, apart from when we find ourselves vertically beneath MSCI World itself, in which case we leave that cell blank.

By way of recapitulation, we would do this by using the Excel correlation function, cutting and pasting first the MSCI data series and then the target comparable data series. It is very important to make sure that we are comparing exactly the same periods. For example, if we come across a return series where data is only available for the previous ten years, we have to make quite sure that we are comparing it only with the previous ten years of MSCI data.

Constructing our portfolio

Now that we have the necessary colours laid out on our palette we can
begin to mix them together to paint our picture. There are specialist
software programs, called optimisers, that will do this for you and these
will be examined separately below, but let us first look at conducting the
process ourselves.

The most important thing to note before we begin is that the asset
allocation process requires above all an open mind, and a willingness to
consider a number of different asset types. We must also, of course, have
agreed our target rate of return and investment time horizon. If not, then
asset allocation (at least properly so called) simply is not possible, and the
discussion will take the form of 'What should our bond/equities mix be?'
baby talk.

Incidentally, it is worth noting at this stage that there are some
schools of thought that entirely disregard asset types, at least as to what
they are, or what they are called, and focus only on how they might
behave relative to certain risk factors or exposures. However, as this is
still regarded as a new and specialist area it is dealt with separately in
Chapter 10.

Now we can start mixing together the various asset types we have laid
out on our palette. This is definitely an art rather than a science, since
there are a potentially infinite number of possible combinations. You can
restrict these substantially, however, if you follow a proper multi-asset
class approach and only consider allocations to any single asset type that
are significant, which, let us assume, means at least 10 per cent. For each
combination you will note the suggested average return and volatility. By
looking for returns that have been lowly correlated you will find it easier
both to increase the former while reducing the latter.

As mentioned above, there are specialist computer programs, called
optimisers, which can do this for you and they can be a useful aid.
However, they have a number of limitations that are not properly understood. Quite the contrary, in fact, as their models and outcomes can
assume an almost mythological stature, the assumptions and methodology of which are never questioned, since it is assumed that a computer
and the consultant operating it must know best.

In fact, an optimiser is subject to a number of restraining factors. First,
and most important, they operate on past data and so assume that past
returns will be a good guide to future performance, whereas a human
team may conclude, after due research and discussion, that some amend-
ment is required in respect of projected future returns, whether for a
limited period or generally.

Second, as we have seen, there are certain asset types for which annual returns are not really a valid measure; a human being will appreciate this, as well as the likely extended pattern of future cash flows, and exercise subjective judgement when assessing the asset class, whereas a computer cannot. Again, this is a limitation of the asset allocation process generally, forced on us by the tyranny of periodic returns. At least a human being can run some sanity check IRR calculations using assumed cash flows, whereas this forms no part of an optimiser's process.

Last, and most important, an optimiser is only a glorified version of the goal-seeker function within Excel. It can work only within the confines of the limits its creator has set for it. So you need to check whether it has been set to ignore certain asset types completely, or to consider only insignificant allocations to certain types.

What this process will throw up, whether or not an optimiser is used, is a short list of a number of possible portfolios, all of which seem to offer something like the target rate of return required at an acceptable level of volatility (for the traditionalists) and at an acceptable level of systemic diversification (for the modernists). Discussion now needs to turn to the particular asset types suggested in each combination.

Deciding between asset types

Just because a particular asset type appears to work well when mixed with others within a notional portfolio, it does not necessarily follow that it is a desirable one for the individual investor in question.

It is here that one needs to refer back to the outcome of the SWOT analysis. Does the organisation have the expertise required to be able to consider certain asset types to an appropriate degree? If it is an asset type that demands the use of multiple managers, some of whom may be raising funds to which there may be limited access and/or for which there may be an excess of demand over supply, does the organisation have the necessary speed and flexibility of decision-making to be able to capture the best opportunities? Is there some regulatory constraint on the organisation that may make it difficult or even impossible to invest in the asset type even if it wishes to do so? What level of headline risk (possible media exposure should something go wrong) exists, and would the organisation find it acceptable?

One hopes these will all be issues that have already been picked up during the initial strategic analysis of the organisation, but the sight of specific asset types set down on paper as potential allocation recipients will serve to focus debate on whether or not it does make sense to proceed with them, or perhaps whether one might proceed in one way but not in another.

This is because, with respect to various asset types, it may be possible to access them in more than one way. We shall discuss this shortly; briefly, it comes down to a debate between what is generally known as active investing, which requires the appointment of various individual managers, and passive investing, which does not. Thus those who say that implementation has no part to play in the strategic process are incorrect. There are some asset types that can only be accessed in a certain way, and the question of whether the organisation is well equipped for that particular mode of access is a valid subject for discussion, since it potentially represents a strength or weakness, depending on the answer.

Another factor that needs to be borne in mind is the risk exposure of the organisation itself. If it is exposed to certain type of risk on its liability and/or revenue facets then it makes no sense to double (or even treble) up on that risk in its choice of investments. Some investors are better than others at spotting this and taking appropriate action. The sovereign wealth funds of some oil- and gas-rich states eschew energy sector investments, yet various social security or pension reserve funds hold the bonds of their own government almost exclusively.

A note on long-term portfolios

As we have already noted in Chapter 4, there is a strong argument for the proposition that within a long-term portfolio, liquidity is at best irrelevant and at worst a positive disadvantage, while volatility is actually a good thing to be sought out, since any long-term investor should engage in rebalancing (see below). However, this is a very difficult argument to make, and can even be a deleterious one in that, to a rigidly traditionalist mind, it can seriously throw into question the credibility of the person making it. Pension consultants and regulators, in particular, seem to operate rather like those in charge of the Spanish Inquisition who took such pride in rooting out dangerous heresies. Many investors, particularly public sector ones, may be likened to the compliant rulers who were happy to allow the Inquisition to operate within their countries, content that dissent that might ultimately threaten their own positions was being summarily stamped out.

So, when presenting asset allocation ideas to an investor, the process best resembles some sort of political juggling act. At the very least, lip service must be paid to the idea that volatility and risk are in some way the same thing, and experience suggests that it is simply not worth pushing the case for assets that exhibit high volatility and/or a low Sharpe ratio.

Fortunately, there are usually plenty of others that do not present such problems. Unfortunately, these tend to fall victim to something called confirmation bias, which makes people expect or seek out data that confirms their already existing beliefs. So, when a Sharpe ratio for an asset they perceive as 'risky' turns out to be an unexpectedly low number then a frequent reaction is either to disregard it, or even to change it (since it cannot possibly be right).

Liquidity is usually less of an issue, if only because it is extremely difficult to put together a portfolio that will not involve a high degree of liquidity. Some type of quoted equity exposure will commonly be present, and exposure to many asset types may today be through either ETFs or other quoted vehicles such as REITs, all of which are, of course, liquid. Indeed, it would be possible, were one so inclined, to put together a multi-asset portfolio composed entirely of liquid investments.

Implementing your chosen portfolio

As we shall see shortly, with regard to many asset types, implementation involves the making of a basic decision as to whether you are going to be content with the return of the asset class itself, which will necessarily be the same for everyone, or go for something different. The latter requires you to take on a specialist in-house team and/or to appoint multiple external managers, whereas as the former does not. However, as we shall be considering this point fully in Chapter 9, at this juncture let us simply note it and move on.

Manager selection is really a subject in its own right, and arguably deserves a book all to itself. Briefly, good advice would be to look beyond the mathematics and consider the 'soft' issues such as the human qualities and dynamics of the team, and the environment within which they operate.

Where managers operate in a field such as quoted equities there is a plethora of devices to choose from which purport to show what part of a manager's return has been derived from the market itself, as opposed to individual stock-picking. It is also possible to analyse to what extent the manager does the latter compared with the former, and to look at the effect of them choosing not to invest (that is, to be holding cash) in whole or in part at any one time. These are all valuable dials on the dashboard and can prove to be useful tools in the selection process. However, you should not allow them to blind you to those matters that cannot be calculated from the historical data. First, there is a strong argument, both from academic research and from practical experience, that the returns of an out-performing manager will go down if a key investment manager leaves the team (particularly if it is *the* key manager), and second that there may be a natural cycle of out-performance pulling in higher amounts of capital, and the manager then struggling to achieve the same results with a large pot as with a small one, capital outflows occurring, performance then picking up again and so on. Note that neither of these is suggested as a firm rule; indeed, there are very few firm rules in investment. They are, however, distinct possibilities which should be considered when examining the available data.

Generally speaking, with managers of liquid assets such as quoted equities, the traditional returns analysis measures work relatively well, and their terms of engagement make a change of manager a relatively easy and short-term affair. Relative, that is, to the managers of less liquid assets, the most extreme examples of which would be such things as private equity, infrastructure, forestry and agriculture, where a combination of ongoing investments and fund terms may make a change of manager all but impossible in practical terms. In this case, a secondary sale of one's fund interest may have to be adopted instead.

It follows that extreme care should be taken when appointing such managers. Track record is an important part of the equation, but only a part. The team's investment model should be tested thoroughly, discreet but deep personal due diligence conducted on the key players, and the team dynamics fully considered. An investor's greatest fear is that the team might fragment, and things such as remuneration arrangements should therefore be fully transparent. Again, it is impossible to propose any firm rules, but human nature being what it is, then a close, collegiate group with roughly equal remuneration arrangements is less likely to splinter than a hierarchical one run by one or two strong individuals, but even this is advanced diffidently, since here have been some very prominent exceptions (in both cases!).

Whatever the situation, one is faced with the prospect of entering into a long-term relationship in which mutual trust and respect will be essential. As when entering into such a relationship in one's personal life, decisions should not be undertaken lightly. Of all the cases in which an organisation has to be honest about whether it really does have the time and expertise necessary properly to undertake a task, this is by far the most crucial.

Incidentally, in cases where an organisation does not have the necessary time or expertise to make a proper job of this, then consultants can prove a valuable resource; as a general rule one should probably choose a specialist one, if available, rather than a generalist. In some areas one might also look to go even further than this, with some variant of a gatekeeper, managed account, or fund of funds manager.

Managing your portfolio

It will, of course, be necessary to monitor your individual manager relationships. This will require regular meetings, but make sure that as far as possible these take place on your terms, rather than theirs. From your review of their investments and divestments you will have certain questions, and the best way of making sure that these are dealt with in a proper fashion is for you to draw up the agenda for the meeting and send it to the manager in advance, so that any relevant materials can be prepared.

Be very clear in your own mind exactly what you are expecting a manager to do within your investment programme. If you are hoping they will out-perform the market then in principle you cannot blame them if they end up under-performing instead in any particular period, because they are doing exactly what you have asked to do, exercising their own judgement in choosing specific investments, and quite possibly importing more volatility than would otherwise be the case. However, if the under-performance should prove to be either severe or prolonged, you may well have legitimate cause for concern and at the very least you will want to discuss in detail exactly how and why these losses have occurred.

So far as the asset allocation itself is concerned, you could adopt one of three broad approaches. First, you could set the various allocations as monetary amounts. This was the way in which a lot of asset allocation was done traditionally; if you were the in-house team you might be told that you had so many million dollars to put to work in your own specialist asset type. The disadvantage of this is obvious. First, as you make gains or losses, the amount invested will go up or down. Second, because it is not set as a percentage of the whole, you can find the amount available being changed abruptly from time to time by the board or committee. In some areas, such as private equity, where money takes a long time to be put to work, and diversification by time is essential, this can raise significant practical difficulties.

A better alternative is to use the technique of rebalancing. In its simplest form, you simply come together once or twice a year to look at how the relative asset types have gone up or down relative to each other, and bring them back into kilter by buying and selling as appropriate. Note that this technique works best when one has adopted a passive approach, seeking broad coverage of asset types as a whole, rather than seeking specific individual exposure.

It is less than ideal when some asset types might be both liquid and volatile while others, such as private equity, infrastructure, timber and agriculture, are less affected by stock market movements and much less easy to liquidate. Should a sudden collapse in equity prices occur, an investor could find itself in the nightmare situation of having to sell illiquid assets hurriedly, with great difficulty and at a loss to rebalance, only to find that within a short period the stock market has gone up again and they are now faced with the impossible task of trying to reverse the process and regain their original exposure.

For this reason, most sophisticated investors who hold illiquid assets use some sort of 'collar' mechanism ('fork' in French) whereby different asset types are allowed to move within a band of percentages of the whole. This allows rebalancing to be conducted in a more sensible and controlled manner.

Whatever the precise technique employed, the arguments in favour of rebalancing are overwhelming, at least for a long-term investor who can choose when to sell. With rebalancing, volatility becomes a friend rather than an enemy, forcing investors to do the right thing (buy low and sell high). It is a matter of simple arithmetic to show that, if the prices of various assets begin and end at the same levels but an investor rebalances as they go up and down in the meantime, money can be made purely out of these market movements.

There is, however, a third option for investors, which is to employ what is known as a trend-following technique. This is usually presented as an alternative to rebalancing. Briefly, whereas rebalancing effectively embraces volatility, trend-following treats volatility with the customary suspicion of the traditional 'volatility-as-risk' school, and seeks to minimise its effect on the portfolio in question.

One of the few things on which most investors can agree is that the prices of many assets seem to move up and down in cycles. We have already noted how pronounced this effect looks in stock market levels since the 1990s. Without wishing to sound in any way dubious, it is perhaps a fact that most investors who are active in the market today began their careers within the last couple of decades and invest predominantly in quoted equities, which leads to such widespread acceptance of the central premise. It is undeniable, however, that many managers who have practised a trend-following approach have produced significant levels of out-performance over significant periods.

There is one important caveat to be entered, though. The sort of 'trend following' approach we are describing here, practised by investors at the asset allocation level, is not the same sort of 'trend following' that is practised by trend-following managers. The latter, sometimes called 'macro' managers, are looking to exploit financial and economic trends, often on a very short-term basis, while the former are looking to track the upward and downward movements of individual asset types on a long-term basis.

The theory is both simple to grasp and easy to implement. One has, say, five asset types including a default 'risk off' or 'risk free' one, which is customarily prime government bonds. Each has a specified maximum allocation level. The investor will plot the current market price of each against its moving average. When the price drops below the moving average, the investor will sell, trusting that this signals the start of a 'down' cycle. When it climbs back above the moving average, the investor will buy, trusting that this signals the start of an 'up' cycle.

The only variable here, and where practice differs between investors, is how long the moving average should be (90 days? 120 days? 300 days?) and whether the investor is always either 'all in' or 'all out' on the one hand, or whether a more phased approach is adopted on the other.

The argument in favour of trend following is that it can greatly reduce the amount of volatility exhibited by a portfolio while delivering equal or better returns. Such an argument can be compelling to those of the 'volatility-as-risk' persuasion, and to investors such as pension funds, who have an equally artificial view of risk (as being the possibility that the actual market prices of their assets may move relative to the assumed net present value of their liabilities). This is not intended to belittle trend following in any way. For many investors, volatility *is* important, and anything that might tend to reduce it must therefore be treated as beneficial. In particular, it may help some investors to invest short- to medium-term capital more efficiently than might otherwise be the case.

For a long-term investor with a more sophisticated view of volatility, the argument is less clear. If volatility is seen as a source of return, then does it really make sense to seek to limit rather than use it? A trend follower would argue that all their approach does is to try to reduce the downside volatility while still retaining the upside volatility. Yet what they give up is the ability to carry on buying (rather than selling) as prices fall, and thus being able to profit from a much longer upward journey in due course. Provided one is a genuine long-term investor, and really can choose the moment when one sells, rather than being forced to, then the old argument of rebalancing being a 'free lunch' has considerable force.

There are two other possible problems with the trend-following approach, at least so far as a long-term investor is concerned. First, some of the asset types chosen do not have particularly strong return-seeking characteristics; corporate bonds would be an example. Second, particularly in periods of market turbulence, investors can spend long periods of time 'risk off', sitting on government bonds and either sitting still or (as at the time of writing) making a loss in real terms.

9
How to Access Asset Types: Selecting Passive and Active Managers

Passive and active investing

We have already seen how traditional finance theory divides the risk of investing in any particular asset into two parts. Specific risk is the risk of investing in that individual asset, so in the case of a Coca-Cola share (stock), for example, it would be the way in which the price of that particular instrument went up and down. In practice, life would be a little more complex, because we would also take into account the dividend income it produced, but let us be deliberately simplistic as this will illustrate the point more easily.

The Coca-Cola Company is also a member of an asset type, a group of similar assets that share common characteristics and may frequently be quoted on the same stock exchange. Again, in practice, things will be more complicated than this because Coca-Cola may be a member of various groups, including the biggest 100 companies in America, the biggest 500 companies in America, some number of the biggest companies in the world, as well as global companies in the same industrial sector. Again, however, let us keep things simple and pretend that they are only a member of one group which matters, namely the Dow Jones Industrial Average, also known as the Dow Jones index or commonly just as 'the Dow'. This is a weighted index of 30 large public companies in America, most of them quoted on the New York Stock Exchange (NYSE).

So, just as the Coca-Cola stock price goes up and down, so too does the Dow, or to put it more correctly in finance speak 'the market portfolio of which it (Coca-Cola) forms part'. The extent to which Coca-Cola goes up and down is what we call the specific risk, and the extent to which to the Dow goes up and down is the systemic risk or market risk, which we met earlier in the book referred to as beta.

Finance theory says that systemic risk – market risk – is always part of the total risk of the asset, so that:

the total risk of a Coca-Cola stock = the market risk of the Dow + the specific risk of the Coca-Cola stock

If the Dow goes up it will tend to have the effect of lifting the price of all its constituent stocks. The way in which it does so is often referred to as 'market sentiment' and this may in turn be driven by things such as economic indicators, political developments and blatantly emotional factors such as the prevailing balance between fear and greed, the feel-good factor and so on.

However, if we are choosing to invest in individual stocks such as Coca-Cola, then it is not enough to think only about the way in which the Dow goes up and down. We need also to examine the behaviour of its various constituents. In other words, we need to think about the way in which a stock like Coca-Cola goes up and down independently of the market as a whole. This is rather more difficult to assess, since it can be driven by two different types of influencer.

The first is the group of factors we have just examined that bear upon the market as a whole. Certain businesses are seen as being either more or less sensitive to certain issues than the average of the market as a whole, and this tendency for individual stocks to go up or down by more or less than the market portfolio (for example, within the capital asset pricing model – CAPM) is sometimes called their own individual beta.

This is clearly an unfortunate choice of phrase, since it inevitably causes confusion with the concept of market risk, which, as we have seen, is also called beta. The official explanation – namely that the market has a beta of 1 (as will, in theory, any share that always goes up or down by exactly the same amount at the same time), whereas specific stocks will typically have a beta of more or less than 1 – shows all too clearly that finance has been seen by many to be merely a branch of applied mathematics.

There is a great deal about the CAPM we could criticise in addition to its unfortunate choice of terminology, not least the various assumptions upon which it rests. However, the one thing we need to be really aware of is that these differences between market behaviour and individual stock behaviour are not just caused by the different ways in which they react to the same external factors, as CAPM seems to assume, but also by one-off events that are internal to the company – for example, a profit warning, the departure of a key executive, or a significant capital market transaction.

Since these are one-off, unpredictable occurrences, then by definition they cannot be factored into a straightforward analysis of historical data, which is the only way in which CAPM beta can be calculated.

Having pointed out some of the flaws inherent in CAPM, we should not, however, allow these to blind us to the fact that the overall concepts of market risk and specific risk (though we might query exactly what we are talking about when we use the word 'risk') are fundamentally sound. In the example we have been using so far, for example, we actually have a choice in practice as to whether we buy stock in the Coca-Cola Company, and perhaps also in some other selected corporations, or whether we simply buy the Dow, which we could do by holding an index tracker fund. Under the first approach, what we might call stock picking, we have total risk, whereas under the second, what we might call index investing, we have only market or systemic risk. These two approaches are known as active and passive investing, respectively.

Active versus passive: the big debate

It is difficult to overstate just how different these two approaches are, or how passionate is the ongoing debate that rages between the 'index investors' and the 'stock pickers'. On the face of it, the choice may appear obvious. If one has either to settle for beta (the aim of passive investing) or shoot for some higher amount (the aim of stock picking), who would not prefer the higher return? By the way, at the risk of confusing you completely, this difference between the beta return and what can be earned by an active manager is called the alpha return.[1]

The answer is that alpha does not have to be positive. It is guaranteed only to produce a total return that will be *different from* beta. So, while you may indeed end up out-performing the beta return of an index fund, you may equally well end up under-performing. In the case of a portfolio of stocks chosen by a manager, we might call this 'manager risk'. Alpha return and manager risk are two sides of the same coin.

Even that word 'equally' may be a little misleading. You may actually be slightly more likely to under-perform than over-perform. Active managers charge significantly higher fees than passive managers, so they first have to out-perform by at least the amount of that fee differential just to match the performance of a passive manager net of fees.

Every professional investor would like to believe in their heart that inspiration and expertise can make a real difference to investment

---

1. For the purists, this is something of a simplification, since return differentials can be driven by different factors, and sophisticated investors will try to examine these individual factors through deeper analysis.

returns, and certainly there are active managers who have regularly out-performed the market. However, once you begin to explore whether they have done so consistently over a long period of time, and with the same team and the same strategy, then things become much less clear.

Certainly logic is against you, as exemplified in an illustration by the great financial academic William Forsyth Sharpe (he of Sharpe ratio fame). Imagine, he says, that you gather all the active equity investors together in a room, lock the doors, and require them to trade with each other all day. Since investing is a zero sum game (for every notional investor who makes a gain, there must be another notional investor who makes a corresponding loss), at the end of the day there will be net zero gain overall but logically about half of the investors will have made a gain and about half will have made a loss. Now, send the ones who have made a loss away, but ask the successful ones to come back the next day and repeat the process among themselves.

Fairly obviously, with each day that passes, a further half of the investors will be winnowed out so that after five days only about 3 per cent of the original total will be left. This, argues Sharpe, proves conclusively that it is extremely unlikely that any single active manager can out-perform consistently over time.

However, in practice, two things militate against the death of active investing. First, no matter how overwhelming some may find Sharpe's logic, there will always be those who cling to the belief that out there somewhere there must be a manager who can out-guess the market. Second, as we shall see, there are some areas of investment for which a passive approach is either inappropriate or downright impossible.

In so far as it may be this book's task to impart advice rather than insight, one approach I prefer is to deal with manager risk simply by avoiding it wherever possible, as the next part of this chapter will explain.

How to decide between passive and active

As part of their SWOT analysis (described in Chapter 5), most investors should have concluded that they have a limited amount of time every year in which to put investment managers in front of their decision-makers. This assumes what sadly has become the typical pattern of a committee or sub-committee, not necessarily part of the day-to-day investment team at all, insisting on taking all manager appointment decisions themselves. Even if they do not require a meeting with each manager before appointment (and many do) they will probably require at least one monitoring meeting during the course of each year, and more if they feel they have grounds for concern (such as the most recent quarterly return having fallen marginally short of some arbitrary benchmark).

Most readers will recognise their own organisation as fitting into this description, but even if you are one of the relatively few investors in the world to whom this model does not apply, you will still find this section of interest since even an investment team that has the luxury of making its own decisions will have a finite amount of time available, and it is only sensible to seek to use that time as efficiently as possible.

Clearly, passive investing requires a lot less of your time and other resources than does active investing. After all, a passive manager has no discretion as to in what they can invest. They are obliged to replicate their designated basket of assets as closely as possible, which renders meetings to discuss why they chose particular assets irrelevant. All that needs to be considered when analysing the performance of a passive manager is the tracking error (the extent to which their performance deviates from the chosen beta measure) and their total costs relative to their available competitors. It is therefore strongly arguable that where there is an acceptable beta available for any chosen asset type, then it makes sense at least seriously to consider taking it, and saving your available time for asset types for which no such beta exists.

What is an acceptable beta?

There are three main questions you will need to ask. First, has the beta delivered past returns net of costs that would at least match your target rate of return? Of course, the past is not necessarily a mirror of the future, but past return levels are a valuable indicator, whether average annual or (more usefully) compound, and a shortfall should at least place you on alert as to why you find this asset type so exciting. Has there, for example, been some structural shift in a particular market or technology, which may mean that future returns could be significantly different? If not, then perhaps you might be better off trying another asset type instead.

Second, is the beta representative? Does it actually measure the performance of the asset type as a whole? You need to consider three different things within this line of enquiry: (1) Does it measure all of the asset? (2) Does all of it represent the asset (a different question, though it sounds similar)? and (3) Does it actually represent the asset type at all?

An example of the first two elements might be the various hedge fund indices. These undoubtedly measure a large number of individual hedge funds, but it is common ground that they do not comprise *all* hedge funds. The answer here might be the common-sense one that as long as the selection is sufficiently large, it probably does not matter very much. However, theses primary indices are not directly 'investable', since to do so would involve taking an infinitely small stake in an infinitely large number of funds. In order to make them so, the number of constituent funds is reduced dramatically to a relatively small sample to create an investable index, which is a sort of little brother of the primary one. It is much more difficult to argue that *this* is a truly representative beta.

Finally, there is the problem of a beta offering not actually having very much to do with the chosen beta at all. This may seem an absurd situation, but one real-life example should suffice to illustrate it.

Many investors have chosen to become exposed to infrastructure through infrastructure exchange-traded funds (ETFs), seemingly a perfectly sensible approach. 'Sensible', that is, until you lift the lid and examine what is inside the box. Rather than infrastructure projects, which is the exposure you are seeking, you will find a bunch of public companies operating in fields such as oil, gas and electricity generation as well as waterworks and so on. In other words, instead of access to the private vehicles (usually partnerships) that undertake such projects and generate fairly predictable cash flows, you have instead bought a sub-set of quoted equity beta, which is almost certainly what you were trying to diversify away from in the first place!

The hedge fund indices also demonstrate the problem of investability, which makes up our third question outlined above. Be aware that a lot of the time you are being offered not the beta itself but rather some alternative way of representing it. Much of this coverage is now 'synthetic', involving a derivative instrument (usually a total return swap) over the chosen index. This in turn raises further points for enquiry, notably whether the derivative instrument has been exchange cleared (so that the exchange becomes the counterparty of last resort rather than the issuer) and to what extent something called negative roll yield (the cost of constantly renewing certain types of derivatives as they expire out of the money) may impact returns. To be fair, this latter problem is rarely an issue with the most recent types of total return swaps.

Where you can answer all three questions in the affirmative, you should strongly consider making use of the various advantages that passive investing offers. In fact, you can attempt to concentrate your manager coverage still further by having, as some investors do, a single beta manager whose job is simply, as the name suggests, to give you beta coverage of any asset types you nominate. This can work particularly well if you pursue a trend-following or managed volatility approach, which we shall discuss below. Again, the things to look out for here have already been covered. You will want to make sure that the beta being offered is both representative and investable, and that the manager's cost of doing so is not unreasonable.

If you decide not to go down this route, then the growth of ETFs has made it possible for you to obtain this sort of coverage yourself and at relatively low cost (though do check this in every individual case – some ETFs seem to have unreasonably large fees). This has, in particular, transformed the situation of the ordinary retail investor, who was previously effectively shut out of various asset types.

It is difficult to overstate the savings in time and resources that can be achieved. For example, some investors may be able to cut back from as many as 20 different managers to just one. Some investors currently have four or five managers in the fixed income space alone, something that seems particularly illogical, given that any alpha that might be obtained must be very small in absolute terms and thus hardly worth chasing.

Incidentally, things such as ETFs also make it possible to create more sophistication and specialisation within your quoted equities programme if you wish. They allow you to over-weight or under-weight certain sectors or geographies, and also allow you to gain coverage of parts of the world of which you may have no direct knowledge or experience. Putting together an active portfolio of emerging market equities is a daunting and complex business, but, on the other hand, buying an MSCI Emerging Markets ETF, for example, is not.

Before we get too carried away by the advantages offered by ETFs, however, we should note one very large disadvantage they have for many investors, namely those whose liabilities are not denominated in US dollars. The overwhelming majority of ETFs are based in dollars, and almost none in sterling. To give just one example, at the time of writing it is not possible to gain exposure to the DAX (Deutscher Aktien Index), one of the world's major equity indices, through a sterling ETF. Therefore, in many cases it is not possible to gain access to the asset type you want through an ETF without incurring considerable currency risk.

In some cases this is not too damaging, where the underlying asset type is in any event effectively measured in dollar terms. Gold and crude oil are obvious examples in which dollar risk is going to be present in any event, regardless of the currency of your particular investment vehicle or instrument. In other cases, ETFs themselves offer a way of hedging currency liability, for example through a long sterling/ short dollar ETF. However, this clearly carries an implied cost which can impact on your returns, particularly should the currency position stay broadly neutral.

As we have already seen, however, there are a number of asset types for which passive investing is not an option, since no acceptable beta exists. We shall shortly consider what these might be, and how we might approach them, but first it is worth thinking about whether we should even be embarking on such a course of action in the first place.

Two common-sense principles are (1) if a thing is worth doing it is worth doing properly or not at all; and (2) don't invest in things you don't understand. Just because these two guidelines are routinely flouted or ignored by investors around the world does not mean that they should be treated in this way. On the contrary, they form an essential bedrock upon which to build an investment strategy.

Of course, they are, or can be, closely related, but let us consider them separately. We can do so fairly quickly, since they fit with things we have already discussed.

First, as we have already seen, there is a great tendency among investors to make a very small allocation to an asset type and pull someone out of a different department (usually fixed income for some reason) to take charge of it. To make matters worse, this person is usually also at a relatively early stage of their career, and thus may know some good general financial theory but have not yet had enough practical experience to learn that (at least outside the world of fixed income) such knowledge often does not serve very well in practice. In most of such cases the investor would actually be better off not venturing into the asset type at all, partly for reasons we have already covered.

Second, there is the issue of specialist knowledge should an investor decide to make a new allocation to, say, active currency. Of course, hiring specialist managers gets around this problem since they, naturally, *will* have the required specialist knowledge to make these investments. However, if you know absolutely nothing about the asset type you will not know which questions to ask during manager selection or monitoring, nor will you be able to ensure proper diversification within your programme. Did you know, for example, that there are three quite different techniques for investing in active currency, and various approaches or specialities within each one?

Two real-life examples from my own experience may serve to illustrate this. In one case, an investor had hired a carry trade currency manager and then later complained that the carry trade did not seem to be a very desirable approach. In another, an investor appointed a convertible bond arbitrage hedge fund manager, without apparently any of the trustees understanding what arbitrage was, what a hedge fund was, or what a convertible bond was.

To a certain extent these shortcomings may be addressed by using external consultants, though this may be of limited help where the generalist pension fund consultants are concerned, since they themselves often seem reluctant to appoint high-level specialists in what they regard as exotic and marginal areas. Investors may find it a helpful general guideline to remember that the person appointing managers should ideally know more about the overall sector within which the managers operate than does the manager themselves. The managers will know all about their own approach and portfolio, but the person who appoints them should have a good knowledge of *all* the managers in the marketplace, together with their track records and team dynamics, as well as all the drivers of performance.

So, in the days of greatly extended availability of beta investing, there is arguably no need for any investor to have any alpha exposure at all, and this should be borne in mind when discussing whether to start hacking your way into the jungle of some hitherto unexplored asset type.

Choosing and monitoring active managers

Background

Before starting to consider managers in a particular area, you should be confident that you have the right level of background knowledge to be able to make informed decisions. It is strongly recommended that you do this before you start holding meetings with potential managers. Managers and placement agents with funds to sell create a great deal of noise and frankly can waste a lot of time, which at this early stage you should be putting to better use. In any event, as a good investor you should be proactive, going out to find the best managers rather than waiting for them to come you.

There are many ways in which you can do this. Industry return databases, for all their imperfections, are a vital resource. Curiously, many investors are prepared to make an allocation to a particular asset type but not to subscribe to the relevant database. Relative performance matters. At the very least, it gives you a starting point for both your analysis and your discussions. If you do not have access to the figures you are at a grave disadvantage.

Do not be too proud to speak to other investors who have been active in the area for some years. Most of the time they will be only too happy to share their experiences and even, when the time comes, to make some manager introductions and recommendations. However, this is generally best done in private rather than in the fevered atmosphere of an investment conference. You should be able to network your way into anything up to about 20 such meetings, particularly if you already have a reasonable profile in other asset classes.

Finally, before you begin to engage with managers and their fundraisers, be sure that you have thought through, discussed and put in place suitable systems for dealing with fund proposals. To give just one example, if you become known as a prospect for, say, private equity funds, it is quite possible that you could fairly quickly start receiving between 500 and 1,000 offering documents a year. It would clearly be totally impractical to prepare a full note on each of these and have it considered by your committee, so you need to have worked out what you are going to do instead.

Manager selection

When you select any sort of active manager the same considerations apply: people, process and performance.

Whenever you invest in a fund you are effectively investing in the people who will manage it. At first sight this might be obvious in the case of private markets, such as private equity or infrastructure, but there is much research to suggest that, even in the area of active quoted equity management, performance can fall off significantly after the departure of a key member of the team.

It is therefore vital to learn as much as you can about the team members individually, and how they interact. Team dynamics can range along a broad continuum from a fairly tyrannical command structure to a cuddly collegiate environment. While there have been some outstanding exceptions, as a general rule most investors feel more comfortable with a partnership approach where several people take the investment decisions, but this should always be carefully probed, since in reality there will almost always be one or two people who have actual authority over the others. Do not rely on what the people themselves tell you, but gather as much intelligence as you can from third parties (former colleagues can be a particularly fertile source).

As we all know, managing interpersonal relationships is by far the most challenging thing that any of us will be called on to undertake, so it is hardly surprising that teams can and do splinter, or even collapse. The time to think about this is before you sign up, not after problems arise. If you do your personal due diligence sufficiently well you will be able to identify which of the team members it would be particularly difficult for the manager to do without, and to designate those people as part of appropriate 'key person' provisions. This is especially important in the case of long-term fund structures such as tend to be found in fields such as private equity and infrastructure, but can be equally valuable in vehicles such as hedge funds. At the very least, they force the issue to the surface to be dealt with rather than allowing it to be fudged or even ignored.

Questions also need to be asked about how the economics of the fund are split within the team. Who participates in any management fee profit? If there is a performance related fee such as a carried interest, who gets it, and how does the vesting schedule work? You will want to ensure that the latter element in particular is shared all the way down the team, since you do not want anyone to be tempted to leave and try their luck elsewhere. Team stability is the one thing wished for most fervently by investors.

Sad to relate, there are investors who invest in funds without even having met all the key members of the management team, much less having attempted to build any kind of personal rapport with them. This, by the way, is a particular problem with the 'investment decision by committee paper' approach. It means that those taking the decision will either never have met the key players at all, or may have met them only once, and fairly briefly even then.

The team's arrangements and actions should be what gives you confidence (or otherwise) in their professionalism and thoroughness. Who makes the decisions? How is the investment committee constituted, and how does it operate? What is the process for taking deals through their various stages? Is there a 'sanity check' at the end? How is due diligence carried out? These are some typical questions, but doubtless you will think of many others.

Key things to look for are how deals are sourced, what proportion make it through the various stages of the process, and what parameters the team use when doing their modelling and analysis. This, of course, feeds back into the 'people' part of the equation. Who does what within the process; and are some team members being overloaded? Or have some been doing the same thing for too long, so they might get bored and leave?

As part of this due diligence you should ask to see sample internal documentation from actual deals worked on, and also ask to be walked through a typical financial model. It remains a truism of investment that 'people + process = performance'. You can get a picture of how well this equation might have worked in the past by examining the manager's track record. The nature of your analysis will be different depending on what sorts of investments your manager makes, but there are two important things to bear in mind.

The first is the object of your analysis. Why are you doing it, and what are you trying to find out? You wish to know how your manager is earning their returns, and how they have performed relative to their competitors. The latter requires access to an industry database, as noted above, or, for those situations for which no such database exists, either comparable data you have gathered from other managers, or the use of some agreed benchmark that can also be applied to their competition.

The former requires you to consider the background research you did into the asset type, and in particular into how its returns arise. You can then look to create a model that seeks to isolate the various components. Again, two real-life examples may serve to illustrate the point.

With active equity managers and/or long-only hedge fund managers (who are essentially the same thing) you will be looking to determine which part of the return comes from market timing and market beta, which part from picking individual stocks, and (if appropriate) which part from picking certain sectors, or choosing certain portfolio weightings.

With buyout funds (an asset type within the private equity asset class), returns can be driven by three main factors: earnings or cash flow growth; changes in the multiple applied to such figures on entry and exit; and the effect of leverage (gearing). The first of these can in turn be split into two, or even three parts, depending on which measure is being used, since earnings growth may be driven either by increased sales or improved margins, and cash flow can be affected by stretching creditors or squeezing debtors.

Whatever factor drives your asset type returns, it is vital that you understand it, since if you do not you will be unable to create an appropriate model; yet another example of why you should not invest in an asset type without some specialist knowledge and expertise to hand.

The second thing to bear in mind is the *type* of return measure you are examining. This is a very fundamental point, which in practice many investors fail to consider. Briefly, there are three main ways of stating investment returns and you need to be very clear about which one you are looking at, and why.

Understanding manager returns

Most managers will try to use an 'annualised' return. For retail investors, this will be the way in which the figures used in fund advertisements have been calculated. It is a simple average, what mathematicians call an arithmetic mean. If you are calculating an average annual return you simply take the returns of every year, add them all up and divide by the number of years, just as you would if you were trying to calculate, for example, the average height of all the people in a room.

Mathematicians, however, argue that, when it comes to investment returns, this measure is not appropriate and we should instead use something called a geometric mean. This is still an average, but calculated differently. Investment returns, they argue, are not finite numbers such as heights or weights, but percentage rates of increase or decrease (positive or negative returns). There is an accepted way of creating an average of such percentage rates, which is by turning each into a number relative to 1 and then multiplying (rather than adding) them together. Then, because we have multiplied rather than added, we apply the root of the number of years we are considering.

So, the geometric mean of annual returns of +6 per cent, +11 per cent and −4 per cent would be calculated as follows:

$$\sqrt[3]{(1.06 \times 1.111 \times 0.96)} = 1.041 \text{ or } 4.1\%$$

Note that if we had calculated a simple average (arithmetic mean) we would instead have arrived at 4.3 per cent.

Do not worry if you do not fully understand exactly what is going on here, but there is one very important point to bear in mind, which is illustrated neatly by the calculations we have just performed. It is impossible for the geometric mean ever to be higher than the arithmetic mean. It is almost always lower, and sometimes quite a lot lower. So, clearly, it matters a lot which one you are considering, not least because managers, unsurprisingly, choose to use the arithmetic mean since it always flatters their performance.

Similarly, it is very important to be clear about whether they have stripped out all their fees and other incidental costs, so that what you are looking at really are the 'net net' figure.

So, your first two questions to a manager whenever they are showing you their track record should be 'Are these figures net after deduction of all fees and costs?' and 'Is this an arithmetic or a geometric mean?'. These two questions alone will guarantee you a reputation as a trouble-maker among managers, and as an investment genius to be watched with interest among your colleagues.

However, both these return measures suffer from a serious defect, which is that neither takes into account the time value of money. They assume that the return of every year has equal weighting, and we know that this is not true. Even if we do not understand why this is so mathematically, we are aware of it on an instinctive level. If we know in advance that we will have to suffer a year of losses we would like to defer that as far into the future as possible, while if we know in advance that one year will show a big gain then we would like that to be as soon as possible, and preferably this very year.

Another problem with periodic returns, such as annual or quarterly, is that they are not based on the actual cash flows that occur during the holding period of your asset but (usually) on its deemed market price.

Thus, if you buy gold at the beginning of one year at US$1,500 an ounce and by the end of the year the market price has gone up to US$1,600 an ounce you will be deemed to have made a positive return of 6.66 per cent, thus:

$$\frac{100}{1,500} = 6.66\%$$

However, you could argue that you have not actually made any return at all, since you have not sold the gold. You paid US$1,500 for it and so far have received nothing back. The gain is purely notional until you sell the gold, and it is most unlikely that when you do decide to do so at some future date the market price will still be US$1,600. It may well be US$,1,800 or even US$1,400, in which case you would have made no gain at all but rather a loss.

Consider if you had bought instead a bond for US$1,500 which paid you a cash coupon of US$100. In both cases you would be said to have made a 6.66 per cent gain, yet can these two situations really be thought of as being the same? Would you rather have a notional return of US$100 that could melt away to nothing (and cannot in any event be realised until the investment is sold) or US$100 in cash today?

The use of a measure of compound return, such as an IRR, answers both of these objections. It takes into account the time value of money by treating the returns of future years as being of less value than the returns of today. In addition, it is based on actual cash flows which, it is argued, reflect much more closely the reality of how an investor views an asset. Such measures are routinely used when pricing bonds. A yield to maturity, for example, is effectively an IRR.

Problems arise, though, when investors get in a muddle, looking at compound returns (such as 'vintage year' returns commonly used in asset types such as private equity) but believing them be 'annualised' or even 'annual'. Again, it does not matter if you do not fully understand the different way in which these are calculated, but be aware that the same stream of returns, even if they *are* all actual cash flows, may return a much lower number in the case of a compound return should losses occur towards the beginning of the series rather than towards the end.

Pulling it all together

The ideas set out in this chapter should, I hope, enable you to have an intelligent discussion about manager selection. The sorts of questions you need to ask (and roughly in this order) are: Is there an acceptable beta available for this asset type? If so, is it investable? If so, how can I capture it most efficiently? If not, am I happy to add this asset type to my portfolio knowing that I will need to select various active managers in order to do so? If I *am* happy to do this, then how might I best go about it?

If you do decide to go down this route, then remember that 'people + process = performance', and look critically to examine all three.

10
New Developments: Trend and Risk-Factor Investing

Investment strategy is a field whose range has expanded rapidly in recent years and continues to do so. We have, for example, seen ever more intricate quantitative models, a growing acceptance of more diverse asset mixes, a greater understanding of so-called 'alternative' asset types, and in some quarters a focus on risk rather than reward. Some of these developments have been sensible and beneficial, but others less so. Two approaches that are still relatively novel merit special mention. One of these is an *exposure-based* investment strategy, which relates to specific types of possible exposure or risk. The other is *trend investing*. The former is largely, though not entirely, confined to indirect investors – those who seek coverage of an area through investment vehicles and fund managers, while the latter is more appropriate for those who seek direct asset exposure.

Exposure ('risk factor') based investing

When looking at the annual reports of various North American investors these days it is apparent that some of them are starting to think of the possible different types of exposure they face (the word 'risk' is best avoided, as it understandably gives rise to so much confusion), and ways in which they might seek to mitigate these through their choice of portfolio assets.

In part this is doubtless driven by a growing and healthy recognition that investment strategy should be based on the particular circumstances of the individual investor, with these exposures representing some of the external threats identified during the strategic process.

In part too, however, this is by the experiences of many an investor during 2008 who thought they had deployed their capital in a sensibly diversified portfolio, only to see the correlation between various asset classes head towards one, particularly as against equity markets. While some of this correlation was man-made (if everyone is buying or selling the same thing at the same time, it is hardly surprising if its market price would head either upwards or downwards as appropriate), it is undeniably fair comment that nobody had anticipated the extent to which correlation (which after all can only be measured in arrears on historical returns) could change so rapidly in so short a time.

For an investor such as a pension fund or a life insurance company, two obvious candidates would be inflation and longevity. (The others, for a pension – exposure fund, are investment risk, interest rate risk and sponsor risk.)

Inflation

It might seem at first glance that it would be fairly straightforward to hedge against inflation. For example, one could buy index-linked bonds, or a return swap under which some form of fixed return is swapped for an inflation-based return. However, both of these approaches are fraught with difficulty, and these difficulties increase mightily if one is looking to implement them on a long-term basis.

The problem with index-linked bonds is that there are very few of them available relative to demand (and no government is going to be so stupid as to create any more of them), so that they routinely trade (when they are available at all) at a premium to par value. Thus by definition they do not provide an inflation return at all, but something less than this, since the inflation return is calculated on the basis of the par value. The longer you look to hold the bond, the bigger this gap will grow.

Of course, this also ignores the effect of taxation. Unless one is a tax-exempt investor as a whole (such as a sovereign wealth fund – SWF) or in part (such as a retail investor buying within a tax wrapper) one cannot even hope to protect oneself against the effects of inflation, at least not directly.

There are two problems with an inflation swap. The first is that it comes at a price, and that price may well be enough to create a gap between the net return and inflation. The second is that any swap creates counter-party risk, although increasingly such instruments may well be exchange cleared. There is actually a third, which is that, as with index linked bonds, demand normally greatly exceeds supply. After all, entering into the variable side of an inflation swap creates an open-ended contingent liability which these days creates considerable difficulties on the balance sheet from an accounting and audit point of view.

A more creative approach might be to think of assets that are likely to hedge against inflation, and here equities are commonly suggested. However, it is extremely unclear whether this actually works in practice.

Certainly it does not do so in the short term. There have been many periods, such as in the UK during the 1970s, when the real value of stock markets fell significantly. Sadly, this is also true in the case of two other candidates: real estate and gold, and perhaps the answer for a long-term investor lies in some roughly equal allocation between all three.

For a short-term investor, the truth is probably that it is simply not possible to cancel out the effects of inflation, but that at low levels of inflation this probably does not matter very much. There again, it is not at times of low inflation that one really needs protection! Yet perhaps genuinely short-term investors such as banks might seek to make more of their own lending to customers at variable rather than fixed rates. Though interest rates tend to lag behind inflation, this might at least offer some offset protection.

Longevity

Life insurance companies have a perfect natural hedge available to them here. Their annuities business sells people an income stream for life. The risk of this business is that people will die later than anticipated, which perfectly offsets the risk of their life insurance business, namely that people will die sooner than anticipated. Other investors are not so lucky, with pension funds being a prime example.

Again, swap instruments are available here, with payments being made to a financial institution based on a pension fund's currently assumed longevity figure, and them making or receiving in return compensating payments should the actual longevity of members turn out to be different. Again, there is clear counterparty risk here, particularly as such arrangements are only of any real use if they endure for many years. However, frequently much of this risk is laid off by the counterparty into the financial markets.

It is difficult to see the attraction of such arrangements for the banks involved, given that actuaries seem to have underestimated longevity persistently over the years. The availability of such instruments appears to be drying up, and the imposition of Basel III type requirements may well hasten banks' exit from the market.

So, what remains? One possibility would be for pension funds to pursue the sort of trend-based approach to longevity as outlined below, though perhaps with targeted minority holdings in public companies rather than by way of direct investing.

Incidentally, we have dealt here with only two of the more obvious risk factors. We shall consider more complex risk factor based approaches at the end of chapter, but it may be worth mentioning sponsor risk at this point.

In the UK, at least, this risk has technically disappeared in that should a scheme sponsor commit one of various defined acts of insolvency then in principle the responsibility for paying at least a base level of pension benefits defaults to the Pension Protection Fund. However, other countries do not have such arrangements, and even in the UK the problem has not been entirely solved, since there is an upper limit on the benefit levels that may be paid to any one individual.

Perhaps it is only right that the British government provided this safety valve for UK corporate schemes, since it was government policy (having trustee boards dominated by directors of the sponsor, and advised in many cases by the sponsor's own consultants) that made it so difficult in practical terms for this risk to be addressed. It is submitted that wherever possible it should be dealt with by way of asset transfers, increased contributions, or the granting of security rather than by way of investment-based solutions, particularly as the only obvious way in which to do this would be to short the sponsor's own bonds or equity, which is unlikely to prove a universally popular move.

Trend investing

So far, we have not really dwelt on direct investing, apart from mentioning that it has been a size-related issue for real estate investors. Yet if we were to talk about current developments in investment practice generally, it would be difficult to ignore a growing shift among some of the world's largest and most sophisticated players from indirect to direct exposure. Led by a few sovereign wealth funds and some of the more adventurous North American pension funds (particularly in Canada), they have moved from buying and developing individual real estate assets such as prestige office blocks to buying businesses (or strategic stakes within them), farmland, timber plantations and infrastructure assets.

This does, of course, set up some interesting new dynamics, particularly in areas such as private equity. Whereas institutional investors were once content to be passive LPs (Limited Partners – fund investors) within private equity funds (though frequently seeking co-investment alongside the fund), they are now increasingly competing with them directly for the same investment opportunities.

In part this is driven by a growing disenchantment and cynicism with investment managers generally, with GPs (General Partners – fund managers) in private equity and hedge funds to the fore. The feeling is that, in many cases, high fees and performance payments are charged, but with little corresponding out-performance. In the case of private equity, this cynicism is exacerbated because true performance can only properly be measured many (perhaps 10 to 15) years in arrears, at the end of the fund's life. At the extreme, there remains a significant and vociferous minority within the investment world who regard private equity as some form of confidence trick designed to rob institutions of their money.

To some extent, LPs have contributed to their own problems here. There has been a tendency to focus on big name brands rather than exciting smaller players, and to focus on the mega-buyout space to the exclusion of other, perhaps more interesting, areas. There has also been far too little understanding of the often dramatic consequences of manager selection, with far too many LPs being content to continue supporting lower quartile GPs. Arguably, all these factors have in turn been driven by far too much capital being thrown into the market, often by LPs with very low levels of base knowledge and understanding. I have demonstrated elsewhere[1] a clear apparent correlation between these higher levels of capital raising, or at least rising fund sizes, with lower levels of return.

GPs would argue that fee arrangements have changed significantly in recent years, but this is only partly true. What *has* changed, in the face of strong pressure from LPs, is the so-called 'waterfall' arrangement, which calculates when and how carried interest (the performance-related part of GP remuneration) is paid,[2] but there has been little significant reduction in (non-performance related) management fee levels since the days of much smaller fund sizes.

Again, LPs continue to contribute significantly to their own problems. It seems unclear, to say the least, why they should focus on making less generous the performance-related part of the remuneration (though let us be clear that this was once very unfair, and fully deserved to be changed) and yet give way so supinely on management fees that are payable irrespective of performance (indeed, even if there is a total loss of the fund's capital) and thus create a clear misalignment of interest. A recent report by Preqin showed that the average management fee of funds in excess of US$1 billion remained at about 1.65 per cent. Yet it seems difficult to see how many of these could not be managed in a perfectly satisfactory commercial way for about 50 basis points (half of 1 per cent).

Fees, then, continue to be a significant drag on performance even with more restrictive carried interest arrangements. Incidentally, in case it is thought that private equity managers are being singled out for special attention, let us be clear that similar reservations are also being expressed in other areas: real estate, hedge funds and infrastructure

---

1. See Guy Fraser-Sampson, *Private Equity as an Asset Class* (2nd edn), Chichester, UK: John Wiley, 2010.

2. See, for example, the ILPA (Institutional Limited Partners Association) guidelines, which may be found online at http://ilpa.org/ilpa-private-equity-principles/.

(all for different reasons) would not be an exhaustive list. It is with private equity, though, that the effects can be seen at their most dramatic. A private equity fund which yields a gross return (before fees, carry and other costs) of 30 per cent (and there are currently very few with any such expectation) might actually give the investor only about 18 per cent net, depending on the precise terms and fee arrangements.

In large part this is because capital is only drawn down from investors as it is needed to make investments, and so in the early years of the fund a 1.65 per cent fee on committed capital might actually represent a much higher percentage of invested capital. In part also because a significant percentage of committed capital will usually end up never getting invested, going instead to fees, deal costs and other charges. (Incidentally, this does demonstrate very clearly the superiority to investors of measuring compound returns based on actual cash flows over time rather than using periodic returns. So clearly, indeed, that it remains one of the great mysteries of financial practice why almost nobody seems actually to recognise this.)

Yet whatever the reason, and whether rightly or wrongly, many institutional investors have come to the conclusion that it is increasingly questionable as to whether indirect investment offers good value for money in many cases. Of course, the issue of portfolio size rears its head again here. Smaller investors often have no option but to invest in pooled vehicles, and sometimes even only a sub-set of these. They have little choice in the matter, but big investors do, and increasingly they are choosing to exercise it.

Peter Drucker once said that there are no threats, only opportunities,[3] and perhaps the fee drag offers such an example, at least for those investors who are large enough and sophisticated enough to be able to take advantage of it.

The last point is an important one, by the way. Sourcing, evaluating and executing financial transactions is highly complicated and demanding specialist work, as indeed is the management of the investment post-acquisition. There is little point in an investor deciding to compete directly with investment management firms unless it is prepared to attract, and keep, the sorts of people who would otherwise be working within such firms. These will usually be people with a background in investment banking or strategic consultancy, and who may well previously have worked as senior level accountants, lawyers or industrial managers.

---

3. Or, more precisely, that any change which seems a threat to a business is actually an opportunity to do something different and profitable. Peter Drucker, *Managing for Results*, London: Macmillan, 1967.

Such people do not come cheap, and this can pose problems for institutions, particularly those within the public sector, because they may frequently have rigid salary caps which are set by people who may know a great deal about government affairs, but very little about investment management. Such people are usually also fixated about the cost of something, rather than its potential value. This is a key issue, about which investors should be very open and honest with themselves as they conduct the SWOT analysis that forms an early part of the strategic process. You should not contemplate stepping into any area of investment if you will not be allowed to hire the necessary people to do it properly, and direct investing is no exception.

It is sad that this cost issue so frequently gets in the way of what might otherwise be a sensible and beneficial development of an investor's activities, particularly as people so frequently get it wrong. What is important, as with all financial analysis, is not the cost of something in absolute terms, but in relative terms. What is the cost of doing something in one way, compared with the cost of doing it in a different way?

Suppose that we are a US$5 billion investor looking to allocate about 20 per cent of our total assets to private equity funds. Once we have US$1 billion fully committed we are going to be paying in excess of US$30 million a year in management fees alone, before we start thinking about the effects of carried interest, fund start-up costs, transaction costs, abort costs and so on. For a lot less than that we could put in place a high-quality in-house transactional team to do the job.

There are in fact a number of possible advantages to doing this. Two are practical ones. We now have direct control over the decision-making process; and we can choose for ourselves those assets in which to invest. Also, many vendors are wary of the political consequences and media coverage that might be involved in selling to a private equity buyer, particularly if the business should later embarrassingly become bankrupt, perhaps throwing many people out of work. A strategic buyer, such as a sovereign wealth fund, who is interested in the asset's potential to generate long-term cash flows, may well appear to be a more attractive option. Private equity GPs are driven by the way in which private equity funds operate to adopt a 'buy to sell' attitude, whereas a strategic buyer will be perceived to be 'buy to hold'.

The greatest potential advantage of all is economic, though. Remember that the effect of the fee drag may well be at least 10 whole percentage points. This hands the direct investor an exciting opportunity. They can offer a higher price while still expecting the same net return, or (more likely) offer a similar price but leveraged with much less debt, thus expecting a similar net return but with significantly lower financing risk.

Small wonder, then, that a small but significant group of institutional investors is moving into direct investing. Indeed, there are a few who are now talking about making *only* direct investments. However, any such programme clearly needs a strategic model within which to operate, just as much as any indirect portfolio might do. Apart from anything else, there are questions such as how many investments to have in order to achieve effective diversification, and how to avoid over-exposure to any one geography or sector. Trend investing is one such possible approach.

Trend investing is a fascinating area for anyone who is drawn to the use of the imagination, because it is very much a 'what if?' approach. It is futurist in nature and consists of trying to identify trends that may shape the future (generally, rather than just financially) and then to think about ways in which investment could be made that would benefit from them. You may have heard the marketing expression 'surfing a trend'. Well, this is the investment equivalent.

To see how it works, let us take five possible trends which such discussions might suggest, and look at ways in which we might try to ride them.

Ageing population

We know that we live in a world whose demographics have changed significantly and will continue to do so. If we take the UK as an example, a parliamentary research paper estimates that, by 2020, average life expectancy will be about 80 (just above this age for women, and just below for men), though this is already starting to look conservative, given rapid advances in medical science. Social factors, such as changes in smoking, diet and living conditions, have also all played a part.

To put these figures in context, the comparable figure for life expectancy at the beginning of the twentieth century was just 50. Two-thirds of people died before the age of 60, whereas now only about 10 per cent do,[4] and there is talk of those born today being able routinely to live to at least 100.

We are only too aware of the adverse affect this dramatically increased life expectancy has had on occupational pension funds. Today not a single FTSE 100 company in the UK has a final salary (DB[5]) pension scheme that is still open to new members. The effect on public finances too has been disastrous. When the Welfare State system was introduced in the UK

---

4. All figures from 'A Century of Change', House of Commons Research paper 99/111.

5. Defined benefit.

after the Second World War, life expectancy was about 69 for women and 63 for men, which meant that expenditure on old age pensions was not anticipated to be significant. Incidentally, this also raises the interesting question of why the retirement age for men was always higher than it was for women, rather than the reverse.

We shall look in due course at what investors such as pension funds might be able to do to mitigate the risk of longevity rising still further. However, if demographic change can indeed be identified as a key trend that will continue into the future, how might we ride it to our advantage? After all, as Drucker pointed out, one person's threat is another person's opportunity. Many businesses now cater specifically to what used to be called 'the grey market' but which seems to have become known instead as 'the Third Age'.

A trend investor would look for businesses or assets that would benefit from a large number of elderly customers. If we look at the country that has the most obvious problem with an ageing population, Japan, we might be drawn to some that are obvious, and others which are less so. Examples in the former category might be specialist retirement travel firms, and care providers such as health centres, home nursing, sheltered housing and extra care accommodation. Some from the latter group could include online supermarkets and department stores (some of which in Japan now specifically target the elderly), mobility aids, and what are delicately termed incontinence products. It is a sad thought that we begin our lives wearing diapers and eating baby food, and that many of us end our lives in a similar manner.

Water

It is estimated[6] that, by 2025, two-thirds of the world's population will lack adequate drinking water. Already, specific countries, such as South Africa, are openly discussing the possibility that they may not be able to supply their population even before that date. So acute may the problem become in the absence of remedial action that there is speculation that wars may be fought in the future over supplies of water, rather than oil.

Fortunately for those who seek to position themselves with this situation in mind, the water industry is already a huge one, with a global turnover estimated at about US$400 billion, which would make it the third largest in the world, behind oil and electricity. Unfortunately,

---

6. For example, by the US charity Blue Planet Network, but its figures are generally accepted by the United Nations and the World Health Organization.

however, many of the largest corporations, those utility companies that actually treat and supply water, are understandably heavily regulated, particularly with regard to the prices they can charge. This may be both desirable and beneficial from a political and social perspective but, equally understandably, many investors are deterred from investing in a business that does not operate within a free market environment.

However, there is another side to this coin, which is that in some countries, such as the UK, water companies are protected from the affects of inflation by being allowed automatically to increase their prices proportionately. In 2012, the Chinese sovereign wealth fund purchased a significant minority interest in Kemble, the privately owned company that controls Thames Water. Towards the end of the previous year, the Abu Dhabi Investment Authority (ADIA) took a significant minority stake in Thames Water itself, while also in 2011 the Hong Kong businessman, Li Ka-Shing, bought Northumberland Water.

Press comment[7] has focused on the stable returns protected from inflation that such investments should provide. While this is true in principle, it must be subject to significant caveats, none of which appear to have been acknowledged.

First, for a foreign investor, the fact that such holdings are denominated in sterling create a currency risk, and if one believes in purchasing power parity (PPP) then any increase in UK inflation relative to other countries will be reflected in a fall in the value of sterling relative to other currencies. Thus an investor will gain in net terms only if inflation in its own country is greater than that in the UK, and remains so.

Second, it assumes no change in government policy – surely a dangerous assumption in respect of politicians, who must always be tempted to pander to short-term electoral popularity rather than long-term economic concerns.

Third, it assumes a stable payout policy; corporate earnings are of little use to a shareholder unless they are actually distributed. Yet Britain's water infrastructure, much of which dates from the nineteenth century, suffers from significant leakage and will require substantial future capital expenditure.

Fourth, one has bought equity risk. Utilities are quoted companies that will move up and down with stock-market beta. For a long-term investor such as a sovereign wealth fund this may not appear to be a huge issue but it does raise the question of the extent to which increases in inflation must inevitably be tracked by similar increases in share prices. To think

---

7. See, for example, *The Guardian*, 20 January 2012.

of an equity investment simply as if it were a bond-like source of steady cash flows is surely both illogical and dangerous.

Fifth, one has bought operating risk. Even if one is comfortable with all the above issues there remains the uncomfortable truth that in the event the business may simply not be as well managed as it might be. In a worst-case scenario it might even be mismanaged into insolvency. This is a particular problem in the case of a minority holding. At least Li Ka-Shing bought total control.

Some investors might therefore prefer to invest either in the infrastructure or technology aspects of water. The former might include those who design, build and operate structures such as desalination plants, and the latter businesses who develop new techniques to aid the conservation or purification of water. This second group might be particularly attractive, as they would often boast ownership of proprietary technology that might operate as a barrier to the entry of others, and would offer an exciting growth capital type of return potential.

Mega-cities

Few might have remarked on this at the time, but in 2008 the human race passed what may prove to have been a very significant milestone indeed. For the first time, half the world's population lived in towns and cities. In the years to come, this proportion will rise steadily towards at least two-thirds, and many cities around the globe will become mega-cities, a term that is currently being defined as having at least 20 million inhabitants.

This clearly raises all sorts of challenges, and it is inevitable that many of them will fall to the private sector, whether by design or (more likely) by default. Much additional accommodation will have to be provided, either by way of constantly expanding areas of new housing, or the replacement of existing stock with high-density buildings. Transport networks, already overstretched and in some place almost non-existent (as in Dhaka and Jakarta), will have to be able to carry dramatically greater numbers of people, and perhaps over much greater distances. The provision of water, electricity, gas, telecommunications, sanitation and refuse disposal will rise to new levels of complexity. What may seem peripheral issues, such as education, health care and law and order will also be thrust to the fore.

In some countries, such as Japan, where the Greater Tokyo area has well over 30 million inhabitants, some of these challenges have already been overcome, at least in part (though not completely, as anyone who has travelled on the Tokyo underground system can attest). In some countries, such as China, where there is a strong tradition of central planning, perhaps some of these problems are already being faced and discussed. In other countries, where politicians enjoy only limited tenure, and where corruption and inefficiency may be rife, they appear to be largely ignored.

It is in Asia, and South and Central America, that the major impact of this trend will be seen. In 1900, the four largest cities in the world were London (already with a population of 6.5 million), New York, Paris and Berlin, with Chicago and Vienna tied for fifth place. In years to come, of these, only New York will feature in the top ten, with the others likely to be Tokyo, Mumbai, Mexico City, São Paulo, Delhi, Shanghai, Calcutta, Dhaka and Jakarta.[8]

Following Drucker's principle, it is here that opportunities are likely to be found, in areas such as house-building, civil engineering and utilities-type infrastructure. Again, it may be particularly advantageous to seek out companies that seem to offer 'smart' solutions to challenging problems in areas such as transport and telecommunications.

Incidentally, it is interesting how many of these themes seem to coincide (and interact) in Asia and South America.

Fuel and energy

This is another interesting area, not least because it is a good example of the need to be alive to structural change. There seems to be general agreement that the world has passed 'peak oil', the point at which future demand growth can no longer be offset by further discovery and exploitation, though this is a somewhat difficult field, since certain oil reserves that are difficult or uneconomic to access at the present time could become viable if oil prices reach higher levels.

With gas, though, important breakthroughs have occurred in the techniques of extracting shale gas, and in their political acceptability. Shale gas is natural gas that is trapped between layers of shale which can be fractured hydraulically (a technique known as 'fracking'), thus releasing the gas. Dramatic declines in the market price of natural gas, particularly in North America, have been the result of shale gas extraction.

While gas is an important source of energy, particularly as power stations with nuclear power have once again become a hot political potato after the Fukushima disaster in Japan, it cannot disguise the human population's reliance on oil and the fact that, in anyone's view, oil reserves must logically dwindle away steadily to nothing.

---

8. See http://www.forbes.com/sites/davidferris/2012/08/31/the-stark-environmental-challenge-of-asias-megacities/.

There are various ways in which this trend might be ridden. Some might choose to take a long position on the price of oil, though this is difficult to do on a long-term basis except through an ETF, and even here there are possible concerns as to negative roll yield (the cost of options continually expiring out of the money) or counterparty risk (in the case of a return swap-based fund).

For the direct investor, however, opportunities might beckon from among companies involved with oil services, particularly those who might have expertise in discovering or extracting oil in difficult areas. Equally, however, they could target businesses developing technology for greater fuel efficiency, or even for sources of alternative energy such as fuel cell technology, or components for electric or hybrid vehicles.

Pollution and the environment

As the world's population grows, so does both its industrial production and its urban consumption, and the problem of what to do with the waste products of both must also grow ever more acute.

On the one hand, there may be investment opportunities in new technology to reduce industrial waste and emissions, or help to minimise or neutralise their effects. On the other hand, businesses that specialise in producing clean energy – for example, by solar or wind technology, would also qualify for consideration. The latter area is, however, a rather difficult one for an investor to evaluate properly, because it has sprung up and become commercially viable in certain parts of the world only because of government subsidies designed to facilitate the meeting of publicly stated targets for the contribution of alternative energy sources to the total generated nationally. While this is fine and laudable in principle, there is a strong temptation for governments casting around for savings in public expenditure to renege on these commitments rather than do something even more harmful, such as reducing the number of civil servants.

Areas such as the recycling industry look attractive, whether it is those providing collection or disposal services, or those producing plant and machinery. Given a choice, the latter would probably be preferable, since the former are usually selling into the public sector, with the possible disadvantages this may entail.

New developments: risk factor parity

Risk factor investing is no longer new, though it is far from universally accepted. Before 2007, for example, some investment managers were offering programmes that claimed to be able to replicate various hedge fund strategies. Adoption of these was very slow, and many queried to what extent they would hold up in abnormal market conditions – precisely the sorts of conditions that promptly ensued.

It is the case, however, that many investors, including both pension funds and sovereign wealth funds, do now openly consider as part of their investment process the risk factors to which they might be subject. This is obviously desirable both in itself, since investment strategy framed in a vacuum without reference to one's liabilities (and thus those factors that might influence them) is meaningless, and at a more fundamental level since it helps to move investors away from the 'volatility-as-risk' mantra. Anything that forces a more intelligent view of risk as a hugely complex phenomenon, so complex indeed that it can almost certainly never be fully understood, is a large step in the right direction.

More recently, some finance academics and investment managers have started to take an even more fundamental approach to risk factors.[9] Traditionally, the idea behind risk factor investing was to balance a portfolio at a given level of a chosen measure, or even to balance completely out all the factors, so that one could achieve 'risk parity', a state in which you have successfully cancelled out all market risk, or more precisely one in which you can invest without having to take any particular view on any particular market.

Such an idea has some exciting implications and possibilities. For example, it must be implicit in such an approach that the nature of an asset is irrelevant; all that matters is how it is likely to behave in your portfolio from a risk factor point of view. A true risk factor parity approach has to transcend arbitrary classification and move beyond knee-jerk reaction to the labelling of assets.

However, investment being more about emotion than mathematics, this requirement also highlights the fatal flaw in the approach. Because investors by and large are *not* prepared to abandon their arbitrary asset allocations. A good example of this can be seen in the case of infrastructure bonds, which are shunned by many pension funds because while they offer many of the advantages of government bonds at a higher rate of return, they have to be put in the 'infrastructure' box rather than the 'government bonds' box. So, while risk factor parity may be fine in practice (note the 'may'), it generally requires too large a leap of faith for many institutional investors.

---

9. See, for example, Leanna Orr, 'Is Risk Parity the End for Asset Classes?', *aiCIO*, 17 October 2012. Available at: http://ai-cio.com/channel/RISK_MANAGEMENT/Is_Risk_Parity_the_end_for_Asset_Classes_.html.

Another problem is that it relies heavily on the use of both leverage and derivatives, and many investors understandably restrict their use of both, particularly since the events of 2007 and 2008. So, the best assessment of risk factor parity investing at present is that the jury is out, at least until some significant number of investors adopt it, run it for some years, and then publish the results. As an idea, however, it is clearly an interesting talking point.

Something particularly encouraging is not necessarily the underlying mechanisms, which are, as even risk factor parity devotees point out, as yet largely untried in practice over any significant time period, but the basic conceptual view behind them. This view is that it does not matter one jot what an asset is called, but only what its qualities might be and how it might perform within your own individual portfolio. One has only to move from that to the next logical step, namely that as no two portfolios are the same, then neither will the result be of joining the same asset with each, to appreciate fully both the awesome complexity of investment strategy and the absolute need for it to be fully and intelligently undertaken. Sadly, though, one has also to lament the fact that it is so rarely undertaken at all.

11
Ten 'Do' and 'Don't' Guidelines

Do have a strategy

It still seems remarkable that one should have to give such fundamental advice, but the sad fact is that, at least in my personal experience, very few investors, even large institutional ones, have ever really gone through anything like a full strategic process, and in consequence are operating without any real, cohesive investment strategy.

If you do not have a strategy it is like attempting a car journey without a map, signposts, a speedometer or petrol gauge; without knowing either your destination or your starting point; without knowing the characteristics of your car; without knowing whether it is either roadworthy or properly insured.

Small wonder, then, that many investors just seem to drift aimlessly along, often 'breaking down' or 'having accidents', and frequently expressing fear about venturing off the motorway on to the less frequented side roads.

A strategy provides a framework within which you can both choose your actions and judge their consequences. Without being unduly cynical, it is perhaps for this reason that many investors choose not to have one. If nobody knows what your objectives are, then nobody can say that you have failed to reach them. In the absence of a strategy, success or failure seems to be about the absolute return of some individual period, often being judged against some arbitrary yardstick, and often expressed in relative terms to the volatility of the returns of past individual periods.

At the very least, you should know where you are starting from and where you are aiming to go.

Do be honest about what sort of investor you are

'Know thyself' is one of the best pieces of advice any investor could be offered. All too often, seemingly impressive strategic plans break down because they turn out to be grandiose or unwieldy relative to the organisation's ability to execute them.

These problems can be prevented if only investors are open and honest in the first place about the sort of organisation they really are, rather than wishful thinking about what sort of organisation they would like to be. Protracted decision-making, heavily bureaucratic processes, lack of specialist knowledge and blinkered thinking are the main factors that typically act to frustrate over-ambitious intentions.

The truth is simple and brutal. If you take over a year to make decisions there is no point in aiming to invest in areas that may require frequent, nimble repositioning. If you not a sophisticated investor, you must make sure you have an unsophisticated programme, relying heavily on available beta and limiting your number of investment managers. The same applies, by the way, to an organisation's outward-facing activities. If you repeatedly perform a great deal of analysis on propositions, only to be unable to make a decision, either at all or within the required time parameter, you will quickly gain a reputation as a time-waster and the quality of opportunities you are offered will decline steadily and rapidly.

The old adage says 'cut your coat according to your cloth'. That your investment strategy should match the circumstances of your organisation is a fundamental requirement.

Do devote most of your time to strategic issues

Despite the arguments that continue to rage over the scope and validity of particular studies, there does seem to be strong evidence that by far the largest part of investment out-performance is driven by strategic-level decisions, such as asset allocation, and a surprisingly insignificant part by tactical-level decisions such as means of access or manager selection.[1] Yet, irrational though it obviously is, most investors in my experience spend almost all of their time considering the latter and almost none of it addressing the former.

This is probably the single most significant change you can make within an organisation. Forcing key decision-makers to focus on 'big picture' issues and honest self-analysis can only lead to better-informed asset allocation. Yet while it may seem to be an easy change to make, in fact you are likely to find that it is fiercely resisted. In part this may be because the need for strategy, as distinct from tactics, is not understood.

---

1. It is acknowledged that there are some significant exceptions to this principle, most notably in private equity.

In part, all-too-human reasons will also operate. Permanently retained consultants, for example, seem to be particularly nervous about having their thinking and advice explored, or the possibility of being asked about specialist areas of which they have no direct experience.

Despite the difficulties, it is necessary to inculcate strategic awareness into an organisation's culture. For many, strategy is an optional extra to be pondered twice a year in a luxury hotel. Even then, what is being discussed is not usually 'strategy' at all, but tactics. It is important for people to be brought to understand that strategy should be an agreed overall framework within which tactical decisions can be made consistently and intelligently. Without such a route map, decision-making can only be haphazard and frequently mutually conflicting.

Do take beta where an acceptable one exists

There are very few investors in the world who are sufficiently large and sophisticated to run an investment programme that consists entirely of alpha-seeking managers or projects, even if they wanted to. Time, in particular, is the most valuable resource of any investor, in the sense that it is always in short supply, particularly for decision-making. This makes it almost compulsory for any investor to seek to minimise the number of manager relationships with which they have to deal, and many investors around the world are in fact currently seeking to do just this.

This in turn strongly suggests that once an asset type has been selected for investment, it is sensible to look to access its beta, provided it satisfies the tests of representation and investability we examined earlier. In this way, not only can the number of manager relationships be restricted to one for each asset type, but the investor may even be able to appoint a single manager to provide multiple beta exposure across a number of different asset types.

If pursued on this basis, the 'active versus passive' debate is immaterial, since the investor would probably not be able to pursue a multi-manager alpha-seeking approach even if they wanted to. However, just in case no such time constraints exist (and they almost always will), it is worth noting that there is little hard evidence, certainly not in the case of academic studies, for the persistence of manager out-performance net of fees over extended periods. In fact, the opposite seems to be suggested, particularly if the departure of key individuals is taken into account. Thus, on balance, a beta approach is likely to cost little by way of returns forgone over the long term.

This particular 'do' assumes, of course, that an acceptable beta is available. As has already been noted, there are some asset types, such as private equity, infrastructure projects and real estate investment in many parts of the world where this is simply not the case.

Do make sure you have a mix of different asset types

As we have seen, no investors would dream of holding an equity portfolio composed of one single company. The concept of diversifying away specific risk is well recognised. However, most investors do not seem to be able to stretch themselves to the idea that systemic risk too ('beta') can, and should, be diversified away. Worse still, there often seems to be a deeply engrained belief that other asset types are in some way naturally 'high risk', whereas in fact using their chosen measure of risk (historical volatility), they are often actually less high risk than their own chosen asset type (typically domestic quoted equities).

As with all products of human emotion, it can be very hard to deal with prejudice. Even hard data can prove to be ineffective, with some investors simply altering figures that do not chime with their beliefs! Strangely enough, such prejudice seems to be strongest among those who have some small knowledge of investment, rather than those who have none at all. Lay pension trustees, for example, usually quickly and eagerly grasp the image of the 'five buckets' approach.

What makes life even more difficult is that the naysayers do have some strength of argument on their side. It is perfectly true that if you look simply at the headline periodic return figures, then correlation between asset classes increased dramatically in 2008. It requires an enquiring and open mind to look behind those figures and, indeed, behind periodic returns, to glimpse the deeper truth.

The bottom line is that sensible diversification should always be pursued, between as much as within asset classes, both to reduce exposure to particular risk factors and to extend the efficient frontier of returns.

Do rebalance, or have some similar approach

Had you settled on an equal distribution between five asset types in about 1990, one of which was private equity, then several years later the private equity portion of your portfolio might well have grown from 20 per cent to over 40 per cent. At different times other asset types, such as gold, emerging market equities or technology stocks would have shown similar characteristics. Left to their own devices, such dramatic fluctuations in return would seriously undermine your approach to diversification.

It is necessary, then, to rebalance, with some of those investments that have performed well being sold to buy more of those that have under-performed. In this way, an investor takes advantage of volatility rather than being hurt by it, and it is a fairly simply matter to show arithmetically that if various assets both start and finish at the same values, but fluctuate in the meantime, then rebalancing is the closest thing to a free lunch that investment has to offer. It only remains to decide at what intervals one should rebalance, with quarterly, six-monthly and annually all being practised.

An exception to this would be a trend-following approach. In extreme examples of this you can be either 'all in' or 'all out' of an asset type at different times, based on technical indicators such as moving averages. Such approaches can be shown to reduce volatility. It is as yet unclear whether they are likely in the long term to out-perform a rebalancing approach, particularly if one is considering cash-flow-based compound returns. In any event, such an approach cannot be used for private market asset types such as private equity, infrastructure funds and real estate (though REITs can in some cases provide a substitute for the latter).

Incidentally, while this is a truth probably better not communicated to your investment committee, rebalancing has another virtue in that it forces investors to do the right thing. If you practise rebalancing you are forced to sell high and buy low; you have no other option. Sadly, experience and behavioural finance suggest that most investors tend to do exactly the opposite, selling an asset type when it collapses in price and only buying it back again when it has recovered to something like its previous high.

Do think globally

Most investors seems strangely reluctant to venture out of their own domestic markets, which may in part show a sensible reluctance to incur currency risk unnecessarily. However, the word 'unnecessarily' is obviously key here, and currency risk should always be weighed against other factors. If you are an American investor then, given that the USA is a huge, homogenous market and that many of the world's investment vehicles, and even whole asset types, are denominated in US dollars, such reluctance may be a defensible approach. If, on the other hand, your domestic economy is small, your government is heavily indebted and/or politically unstable, and your currency is fragile, it may potentially be suicidal.

This shows itself most obviously in the area of real estate. Most investors, if they have any allocation to real estate at all, tend to invest exclusively domestically. Only the very large investors tend to be exceptions to this rule. In former times, when it was difficult and/or expensive to invest other than directly in bricks and mortar, this was perhaps understandable. Today, when REITs, private fund vehicles and even synthetic exposure are all available, it is much more difficult to justify.

The reason is that real estate returns around the world vary in their correlation both against other real estate returns but also, and crucially, against their domestic equity markets. So, in some markets, real estate would at most times have been a good diversifying asset for the local stock exchange, showing roughly similar average performance but lowly correlated returns. However in others, particularly in some Asian locations, correlation between real estate and equity returns has been much higher, so that, to achieve proper diversification, property assets in a foreign market would have been required. One of the many problems that became apparent during the Asian financial crisis of the late 1990s, for example, was that many investors were caught holding both local equities and local real estate (and sometimes having used one as the security for borrowing to buy the other) when both crashed together.

A failure to think globally can, of course, also blind you to a range of possible risk factors, a theme we shall develop below.

Do recognise the importance of time

We have already touched on the importance of time in the sense of an investor needing to recognise just how long and/or how flexible their investment time horizon might be. However, there is another aspect of time that is at least as important, and that is the time value of money, which can only be measured by using compound returns.

Traditional return measures, such as annual returns, do not take this into account, even when the more mathematically 'correct' method of the geometric mean is used. On the contrary, they assume that the return of every period is equally important. Yet we know that this is not so. Anyone given a choice of a stream of cash flows that either began or ended with a large positive number would choose the former rather than the latter.

Nor do they reflect the practical reality of an investor holding an asset. What the investor will be concerned with are cash flows: a negative one when they buy the asset, a positive one when they sell it, and, depending on the type of asset, a series of smaller positive ones in between. The question of what the asset is notionally 'worth', in the sense of what the market is willing to pay for it at any given moment, may be of acute interest to auditors and regulators, since they seem to find such things to be of vital importance, but this has little or no relevance to a long-term investor. Yet traditional return measures are based almost entirely on such artificial 'mark to market' valuations rather than the actual cash flows generated by the investment over its holding period.

Finally, let us remember that there are certain asset types, such as bonds, private equity, infrastructure projects and many types of real estate investment, for which annual returns are already recognised as not giving a valid result; the key number for a bond, for example, is its yield to maturity, which is a compound return calculated on projected cash flows. So, persisting in the blanket use of periodic returns, for example, annual, makes it impossible to compare different asset types validly against each other.

Yet this seems beyond the mindset of the investment community as a whole, with annual returns being used as a yardstick both of institutional performance and the track record of individual managers. Is it cynical to suggest that this may be because compound return numbers will always be lower, and thus generate less of a feel-good factor?

Do invest to achieve your key objectives

This is really an extension of the first principle stated above: 'Do have a strategy'. By far the most important part of the strategic process is to identify the investor's key objective. What is the one thing which it cannot afford to fail to achieve?

Note that the importance of this goes well beyond the world of investment. It is the fundamental factor in *any* strategic process. Suppose, for example, that the target return calculated by a pension fund to meet its liabilities as they fall due is so high as to be impractical? This obviously prompts consideration of actions that lie beyond asset allocation and manager selection. Perhaps the sponsor can be pressed for a supplemental contribution, or prevailed upon to transfer some property assets into the scheme? Perhaps the rate of member contributions can be raised? In the last resort, perhaps the level of benefits could be reduced, or the final salary scheme closed down completely? Incidentally, though this is not generally recognised, DC (money purchase) schemes should be pursuing this sort of analysis every bit as much as DB (final salary) schemes.

Having calculated the target rate of return, it would then be crazy to ignore it. The whole point of having it is for it to serve as your investment benchmark. As a general rule, accept asset types whose return pattern suggests that they are capable of exceeding the benchmark and reject those that seem unlikely even to match it. This approach runs into trouble through emotion, however, not faulty logic. Faced with a portfolio whose constitution resembles nothing they have ever considered before, many investors find it easier to reject this as a ridiculous construct rather than accept it as a logical imperative.

In a sense, the target rate of return is all that matters. If you fail to achieve it over time, you will have failed your exam.

Do consider all relevant risk factors

Considering the various threats that may face your organisation is as important as calculating your target rate of return. Achieving the latter will be so much easier if in your asset allocation you can also take some steps to hedge against the former. By far the most obvious example of this is an insurance company selling life policies to hedge the longevity risk on its annuity business.

As we have seen, some modern investment approaches take the view that risk factors are all that matter, and that perhaps these might even all be hedged away to create a risk parity 'absent the market' environment (assuming the absence of market risk). It is uncertain how many investors will be prepared to go quite this far, especially given the high rates of leverage and derivative exposure required, but ongoing pressure in this direction can only be useful.

First, it helps to educate investors that labelling and choosing assets purely by their apparent physical characteristics is a mistaken approach (see below). Second, it helps to teach them that certain types of investment return and risk factor are in effect different sides of the same coin, so that it is just as relevant to consider one as the other, and preferable to consider both together.

Don't have more liquidity than you need

Liquidity is very expensive, since it comes at the price of lower long-term return expectations. So think of it as a luxury item within your portfolio. You should have as much of it as you really need, but no more.

If you are an extreme version of a short-term investor it may well be that you require 100 per cent liquidity, but such examples are only likely to occur in the case of banks, non-life insurance companies and corporate treasury departments, and even then not universally. It is much more likely that most investors, with pension funds being a prime illustration, will be some mix of short- and long-term, with the flexion point being determined largely by internal policy or external regulation.

Whatever the case, it is important to be clear about exactly where this inflexion point is so that you do not stray into holding excess liquidity. Remember that your liquidity pool can constantly be topped up, perhaps on a quarterly basis, with new liquid assets being substituted for those that have just been turned into cash.

There tends to be an unthinking assumption within many investment institutions that liquidity must always be a good thing, and that accordingly one can never have too much of it. This is simply wrong. Liquidity has a particular purpose, which is to allow assets to be turned quickly and easily into cash. Thus the amount of liquidity you hold within your portfolio should be determined by your likely short-term or unpredictable cash requirements and nothing else. Liquidity is an expensive luxury and it is irrational to hold more of it than you need.

Don't accept lesser degrees of liquidity

This point is really the flip side of the previous one. If you understand why you need to have liquidity, you will realise that it is imperative that it should be real liquidity, total liquidity. What do we mean by that?

Human beings show a strange reluctance to learn from their earlier mistakes. As the political thinker, Edmund Burke, is reputed to have said, those who do not know their history are destined to repeat it. When financial markets faced the threat of a global meltdown in 2008 (particularly immediately following the collapse of Lehman Brothers in September 2008), investors around the world suddenly discovered that they were sitting on supposedly 'liquid' assets that actually could not be turned immediately into cash after all, certainly not at anything like their internal book value. Corporate bonds were a case in point.

It is hoped that we have learnt from those events that if you do need liquidity you must make sure that it is real liquidity. Into this bucket cannot be put even cash any more, for 'cash' is not chests full of banknotes locked in the office basement, rather it is electronic deposits within banks, and as we all know from 2008, banks can and do crash, entailing at best a long wait for your money and at worst the possible loss of all or part of your deposit.

Thus real liquidity can only take the form of what are generally recognised by the term 'prime bonds' – government bonds issued by a very few governments, such as the USA, the UK, Germany and Japan – though in theoretical terms it must now be highly arguable as to whether any of these instruments are genuinely 'risk free'. Gold, sadly, must be ignored, since it can be very volatile in the short term.

The problem that arises is that people persist in talking about 'investing in' bonds, and this raises a fatal misunderstanding. Prime government bonds should not be thought of as 'investments' at all. They are simply cash substitutes held for reasons of liquidity. As such they may not be ideal, but they are the best we currently have.

Don't believe that volatility is necessarily a bad thing

If you have read this far you will know that it is my firm view that the idea of 'volatility-as-risk' is a fatal misconception that lies at the heart of many of our problems as we grapple to turn financial theory into investment reality. To go more deeply into this debate would probably require a book all to itself, so let us restrict our discussion to whether volatility is a 'good thing' or a 'bad thing'.

The answer is that it all depends. It depends, in short, on whether you are a long-term or a short-term investor, either in total or in respect of the part of your assets (or, more correctly, liabilities) you are currently considering. In general, volatility will be a bad thing if you a short-term investor, since here your motive in holding assets is primarily to be able to turn them into cash. In this case, you want to have as much certainty as possible that you will be able to do so when the time comes, and receive a cash sum as close as possible to the amount you originally paid for them.

If you are a long-term investor, however, then you are holding assets primarily for the return they may generate and, assuming that you are pursuing either a rebalancing or trend-following approach, the more volatility you encounter, the greater the potential for return. The one vital difference between these two situations is that, in the latter case, you can choose the moment when you sell (in which case you would prefer it to be on the crest of a very big wave) whereas in the former you cannot (and if you are forced to sell in the trough of a wave then you would prefer it to be a very small one).

What the myth of 'volatility-as-risk' engenders is an instinctive belief that volatility itself must always be an undesirable thing, partly because the everyday meaning of 'risk' is something such as 'the chance that something unpleasant or unwelcome may occur'. As we have seen throughout this book, this is simply not the case. It may be, or it may not be, undesirable, and it is important to be able to tell the difference.

Don't be too quick to label things

Perhaps more damage is done to the asset allocation process by labelling than by any other factor. Let us take a single example, namely infrastructure. On the one hand, it can lead to infrastructure being squeezed into the 'private equity' box even though its risk and return characteristics are entirely different, just because the investor has an agreed allocation to private equity but not to infrastructure, and it might operate through a similar-looking fund structure. On the other hand, it can be rejected by the investor's fixed income department because, despite having the same cash flow characteristics of a bond (but probably offering a much higher return), it is 'infrastructure' rather than 'bonds'.

One of the most important principles of investment to understand is that all that matters is how an asset is likely to behave within your portfolio. It matters not at all what you might choose to call it.

Don't use peer benchmarking

If you understand that the most important requirement of your investment strategy is that it should be aimed at achieving your target rate of return, and this should be a calculated number based upon your forecast liabilities, then you will already recognise how inappropriate peer benchmarking is. It is, however, more than just inappropriate, it can be silly or downright dangerous.

An example of silly behaviour can easily be found in many parts of the world where pension funds benchmark themselves against each other. This presupposes that all of them have exactly the same target rate of return and investment time horizon, which cannot possibly be true unless all of them have identical maturity, membership demographics and funding circumstances as each other. Hardly likely! It also, of course, presupposes that the benchmark, which is almost certainly one that has been arbitrarily selected, is an appropriate one in the first place for even one of the individual funds that might enjoy broadly average circumstances.

An example of dangerous behaviour may be found in a country of my acquaintance which split its public pension provision between six multi-managers to gain a good spread of diversification of asset types and single managers. These multi-managers were tasked with matching the benchmark on pain of being required to make good any shortfall out of their own resources. There was, by the way, no reward for beating the benchmark successfully.

The chosen benchmark was the average of six to whom mandates had been granted. What do you think was the outcome? Yes, of course. They all invested in broadly the same things, thus leading to a concentration of asset coverage and manager risk, exactly the opposite of what the pension regulator had claimed to want to achieve.

Don't follow the herd

This is easy advice to give, but more difficult to follow! It is also important to understand what is being proposed, and what is not.

If you are a short-term market trader, there does seem a lot of evidence that you actually *should* follow the herd, provided you can be an early follower or, better still, try to predict in advance which way the herd will rush. John Maynard Keynes was one of the inventors of momentum investing and gave a graphic notional illustration.[2]

Imagine you are judging a beauty contest, he said, in which five women will be selected to go forward to the next round. You have two choices. You could simply choose those five women you think should win. Better still though, if you replace the contestants with investments, to choose the five you think the other judges will select.

For long-term investors considering asset allocation, though, the situation changes. Here, if you follow the herd you are likely to find yourself in asset types into which a lot of capital is pouring, which is likely to depress returns, with little influence or bargaining power with managers should you decide (or have) to invest actively. Asset types that are out of favour, on the other hand, are likely to be towards the bottom of a price cycle, and certainly not in a bubble.

As David Swensen advises,[3] seek out opportunities in 'less active' markets which, he notes shrewdly, are likely to feature illiquid assets.

Don't discourage questions

Far too many investment approaches run on to the rocks because they fail to change with changing circumstances. This is much more likely to happen within an organisational culture that discourages questions, particularly if one dominating individual is in charge of the process.

Constant questioning should be seen as an essential part of the process. Indeed, some private market investment managers appoint two or three members of the team who have not been personally involved in evaluating a particular fund or project to act as professional devil's advocates before any decision to invest is taken.

Yet this is just as important on an ongoing basis with existing investments, and with asset allocation as well as individual decision-making. Better still, an environment which welcomes questions that are as outwardly stupid as possible, since every so often one of these turns out to be a very good question indeed, throwing doubt on a basic assumption that has gone unchallenged for too long.

Sadly, this rarely happens, and trustee boards in particular tend to sit mute, afraid that by asking what might be seen as a stupid question they will damage their own perceived status in the eyes of their colleagues.

---

2. John Maynard Keynes, *The General Theory of Employment, Interest and Money*, London: Macmillan, 1936, ch. 12.

3. David Swensen, *Pioneering Portfolio Management*, New York: Pocket Books, 2009.

This is a shame, because 'What do you mean by risk?' in particular is usually a killer.

Don't rely too much on mathematics

Those who study for a qualification such as Chartered Financial Analyst (CFA) or an MSc in Finance tend to emerge clutching Brealey and Myers' *Principles of Corporate Finance*[4] in one hand and an engineering calculator in the other, believing that between the two they have the answer to every question that is ever likely to be asked of them in their financial career. Specifically, they believe two things. First, that there is one right answer; and, second, that given the right data and the right financial formula they can calculate it mathematically. Tragically, usually neither of these things is true. More tragically still, many of these people go through their entire careers without realising it.

This is not to decry the value of mathematical processes within finance and investment, nor to deny that they actually work very well in some areas. In the realm of fixed income instruments, for example, mathematics tells you a large part of what you need to know. Yet even here, subjectivity intrudes. To calculate the price of a bond you need to use a discount rate (or the yield, which is the other side of the same coin), and this is based largely on the issuer's credit rating. Yet that rating itself is essentially subjective, albeit reached with the aid of a range of complicated models.

The important thing to remember is that mathematics will supply the readings for many of the dials on your dashboard, but any driver who looked only at his dashboard would crash into a tree at the first bend in the road. Investment is as much about subjective judgement (and, necessarily, about emotion) as it is about logic. It is also as much about conceptual analysis as it is about mathematical calculation. The danger is to believe that, just because you can calculate the standard deviation of the historical periodic returns of a particular asset, you know how to define and delineate its risk. You can't, or at least not unless you can first answer that pesky little question: 'What do you mean by risk?'.

Don't believe the past is always a good guide to the future

A mistrust of an overly mathematical approach should also embrace a mistrust of the past as a guide to the future. It is a well-known truism that

---

4. Richard A. Brealey and Stuart C. Myers, *Principles of Corporate Finance* (10th edn), New York: McGraw-Hill, 2010.

nobody would try to drive a car by looking only in the rear view mirror, but it is remarkable how many investors try to do exactly that.

Any calculation of 'volatility-as-risk', for example, can only make use of actual past data; nobody would dream of doing it with forecast future data, though in at least one sense this might be a more rational approach.

Any criticism of over-reliance on the past must, of course, be tempered by a good dose of common sense. After all, past data is all we have. We use it to calculate things such as volatility and correlation because we have no other way of doing it. Yet once again we come back to the analogy of dials on the dashboard. If you have a trip computer in your car it will indicate the time remaining until you reach your destination, but this is not the actual time that will elapse, since it is a simple calculation based on your average speed to date. The actual time you will take will be some period more or less than this.

So while, we use historical data because we have to, do not fall into the trap of believing that the future will be a perfect repetition of the past. It is far better to try to discern broad trends, and consider whether systemic shifts may have taken place that make them more or less likely to repeat themselves. For example, if you were to calculate the possibility of France and Germany being at war with each other in at least one of the next 10 years based on past data and something called binomial probability you would get an answer of something like 70 per cent. An intriguing possibility. ...

Don't believe that normal distribution will always apply

More fundamentally still, much mathematical financial analysis rest on an assumption that something called normal distribution (or Gaussian, for the 'quants' out there) always applies. Normal distribution is what produces that nice bell jar shape with which we are all familiar, with the vast majority of observations clustering around the average (mean) and becoming steadily and rapidly less frequent the further away from it one moves. It is the tightness of this clustering that we measure and express by its standard deviation. It is one of the great comfort blankets of financial theory that normal distribution can always be relied on to produce the goods.

Except, of course, that it can't. To use just one example, given by Niall Ferguson in his book *The Ascent of Money*:[5] if normal distribution applied, then the Dow Jones index would only drop by 10 per cent or more in any one year about once in every 500 years, whereas sometimes it has

5. Niall Ferguson, *The Ascent of Money*, London: Penguin, 2009.

happened on average every five years. A drop of 20 per cent would be almost impossible statistically, yet it has happened nine times in the last century. On one day alone in 1987 it fell by 23 per cent.

Those of a mathematical bent find such data so disturbing that they can only deal with it by ignoring it. After all, if we don't have the mathematically calculated single right answer to every financial question, what are we to do? Chaos and emptiness would reign.

Well, yes, actually, that would be the case. In large part, chaos and emptiness is exactly what finance and investment are all about. Chaos in that outcomes are derived largely from behavioural factors, such as the ones described earlier, and these cannot even be predicted, let alone calculated in advance. Emptiness if you are looking for some objective quantitative framework within which all investment outcomes can be contained, as most of these will actually have been operated upon and produced by subjective, qualitative factors.

Less so if we start to look at some of these things as being in the nature of the familiar dials on our dashboard, which we can use at least for rough guidance, particularly if we can interpret them in combination with each other and our perceived current reality, and most of all if we can remember that broad guidelines is all they are.

Even less so if we embark on our journey with a detailed map, an accurate fix on our starting point, and knowledge of our destination and how long we have in which to complete our journey.

This book has, I hope, given you some idea of how you might at least start the process of drawing up your map and gaining this essential knowledge. It is not a step-by-step workshop manual, because such a thing is unlikely to be possible. The human and environmental elements of investment organisations are almost certainly too complex for that, and instinct and intuition can only be learnt, not taught. Yet a grasp of the various steps within the strategic process that need to be negotiated in turn, always remembering the feedback loop if necessary, will at least lead to the right people sitting down at the right time and asking each other the right sorts of questions, and it is only out of such questions that strategy can be made.

It is a process which is itself a journey, and one upon which I have embarked, though in some cases *tried to* embark might be a more accurate description, in a number of different situations. As the previous sentence suggests, the results have been variable, with some investors being much more responsive and appreciative than others. Whether one likes it or not, human factors do inevitably get in the way, and if you encounter a senior individual who is simply totally unwilling to have his or her assumptions challenged or in some cases to allow any meaningful discussion at all, then there is nothing you can do except to sit silently and indulge in idle fantasy of their chair suddenly falling through a hitherto unsuspected trapdoor into a tank of piranhas beneath.

Yet on the occasions when it does work well it can be hugely rewarding at a personal as well as an organisational level, with some people openly admitting that they have found a change of approach a liberating experience. Good results will not always follow naturally from good strategy, since there are so many unforeseen events that might occur, but they are likely to do so, and, more important, they are infinitely more likely to emerge from even a mediocre strategy than from a programme that has no proper strategic basis at all.

So I do hope you will be inspired to sit down with your colleagues and start asking a lot of stupid and, better still, awkward questions. I also hope you will find yourself among like-minded individuals who will welcome the atmosphere of intellectual challenge you are creating. If not, you are probably best advised to bide your time while you acquire a saw, some hinges, a tank and some piranhas.

12
Concluding Thoughts: Where Are We Going?

The necessity of constructing a route map has been a central theme of this book. Also, establishing both where we are going and where we are starting from are key functions that the investment strategy process is designed to perform. In addition, of course, we have to know what resources (modes of transport?) are at our disposal, what threats (obstacles?) could make our journey more difficult and, perhaps most important of all, how long we have to complete it.

Yet, in real life, as so often, practice proves infinitely more difficult than theory. One reason for this is that, as we proceed along our planned route, the landscape is constantly changing, and often in ways that, try as we might, we would have found difficult to anticipate. So, we may have planned to take a particular route only to find it blocked by a fallen tree, or crowded to a halt by traffic jams. To carry the analogy further we might even find ourselves stopped and turned back at a police road block (regulatory and compliance issues), be attacked by a mob and have our car set on fire (terrorist risk), or have the vehicle confiscated at the frontier by customs officials (political risk).

Theory can usually do a reasonable job of analysing these factors and working out ways of addressing them once they have actually occurred, but would life not be so much easier if we could predict them in advance?

Well, yes, of course it would, but equally obviously, it would be impossible. The very thing that makes investment so exciting or so frightening, depending on your point of view, is the human inability to see into the future, at least to the extent of predicting exactly which events will occur and when, not to mention how they will arise or with what degree of severity.

We can, however, sit down and indulge in a healthy dose of futurism, trying to identify broad trends that might help to shape our environment, and, as mentioned in Chapter 10, there are those who even make this a central part of their investment approach. In addition, however, we need to understand trends within the world of finance and investment itself, and in bringing this book to a close it might be helpful to set out a few thoughts in this area. It should be stressed that these are the personal musings of the author, but based on both casual conversations and more formal presentations from many professional investors and investment managers.

An ongoing shift from alpha to beta?

Most observers agree that the period since 2008 has seen a significant decline in the number and size of alpha-seeking mandates, and a corresponding increase in beta investing. Hard numbers are hard to come by and would in any event become obsolete almost as soon as they were published, but at a recent Think Tank event[1] it was suggested that, before the crisis erupted, probably about 70 per cent of investment capital was seeking alpha and 30 per cent beta, but that since the crisis those numbers had probably reversed. Certainly, that would be consistent with my experience since then, based on dealings with investors, managers and fundraisers. It is undeniable that a certain scepticism has crept into relationships with active managers, both current and prospective, fuelled perhaps by a growing concern about fee levels and a recognition of just how severely these can have an impact on net performance.

This shift has been facilitated by a growing availability of beta vehicles, most notably ETFs, and by exchange-cleared derivatives greatly reducing the underlying counterparty risk of synthetic ETFs. However, there are still large gaps in the overall coverage, particularly for those whose liabilities are denominated in some currency other than US dollars, and it is to be regretted that no ETF manager seems inclined to position his/her firm as a niche player, preferring instead to compete in already crowded spaces. It seems unlikely that such a situation can continue, and so significant consolidation may be expected.

For those whose liabilities *are* in US dollars, or some closely linked currency, the opportunities are so plentiful as to be almost bewildering. Quoted equity, bond and commodity exposure beta is all cheaply available. Real estate, hedge fund and active currency types of returns can be sourced, with some reservations, through what might be called quasi-beta instruments. In fact, it is probably easier now to think of those asset types where beta is *not* available. Of those commonly considered by institutional investors, they would comprise private equity, infrastructure, timber and agricultural land, and oil and gas royalties.

---

1. Demos Finance, hosted by Nomura, October 2012.

It is not just the range of available betas that has increased, but also their level of complexity. Quoted equity, for example, can at one end of the spectrum be enjoyed globally using an index such as the MSCI World, or at the other extreme through country-specific vehicles. It can also be restricted to high yielding income stocks, or broken down by sector. By mixing and matching, it is now possible to create a portfolio of equity beta that reflects any macro view you may wish to adopt.

Most exciting of all for the time-scarce investor, these vehicles can all be accessed either directly or through a single beta manager. Even here, the word 'manager' would hardly be appropriate, since all that would be required are dealing and custodian services. For a long-term investor, the world of 'push-the-button, fire and forget' investing has truly arrived. Which also means, of course, that, given satisfactory custodian arrangements, manager risk is no longer a valid concern.

It does seem likely, then, that the world of investment will increasingly be built around investors seeking beta exposure where they can obtain it, perhaps reducing their manager relationships in all these areas to just one dedicated settlement and custody platform, and focusing their time and other resources on areas where coverage can only be gained through active managers or (see below) direct investing. However, we must be careful not to treat the world of investment as a homogenous whole. Different investors will move at different paces, and some may even not progress at all.

Will there be a bar-bell effect?

One possible consequence of the shift from alpha to beta and of investors moving at different speeds might be the development of a bar-bell effect both for investors and managers.

There has long been recognition that a certain portion of the world's investors might be termed 'sophisticated'. For securities law purposes – for example, in the USA – the distinction has always been based around status and size; with certainty being a desirable and prized aspect of any law, it is difficult to see how any definition could work otherwise. For investment purposes, however, we need to be subjective rather than objective, and in any case reality is uncertain and shifting, rather than clear-cut and immutable.

Ironically, when we look not at what investors are but rather at what they do, we discover that some of the world's largest institutions may be numbered among its least sophisticated investors. So yes, many large investors would generally be acknowledged to be 'sophisticated' but many would, equally universally, be reckoned not to be.

Foundations, endowments and family offices are generally at the leading edge of investment thought and practice. So are some sovereign wealth funds, but not all, and here the age of the organisation often seems to be a factor. Those that have been around for many years are now supplying many of the industry's thought-leaders, while some of those that are newly formed are as yet not even permitted to invest outside their own country. Pension funds too have to be treated on an individual basis.

What does it take to be 'sophisticated'? Certain common qualities can be discerned: an openness of mind; resistance to arbitrary benchmarking; eagerness to embrace a range of different asset types; and willingness to hire specialist staff to cover them. And decision-making that is as far as possible structured on corporate lines and operated by executives, rather than based on the structure of a public body and operated by committees often composed largely of outsiders.

Since we are dealing here with nebulous concepts based on personal views, it is impossible to state the position with any factual authority. However, it does seem to me that while in recent years those who are already sophisticated have become even more so, the number of those moving up to join them from the ranks of the unsophisticated has been relatively insignificant. It may well be that the renewed obsession with rules-based regulation, requiring those in authority to spend most of their time not doing their job but rather worrying about a myriad of compliance issues, may well have been a significant factor here.

If this view is even partly correct, then investment managers must plan for a world in which investors may occupy either end of an increasingly long barbell, with these two sets of investors perhaps having very different needs and wants.

Those at the unsophisticated end will restrict their activities to their traditional asset types of bonds and equities, though they will probably continue to distract themselves with sporadic and cursory contemplation of what they will continue to call 'alternative' asset types, and may even make a few minute allocations in such areas, perhaps in the range of 1 per cent to 3 per cent. Needless to say, these will not be seen as part of any cohesive investment strategy but rather 'because we thought we should have some diversification'.

Opportunities here will arise within the traditional asset types, since such investors are still likely to be swayed by the siren call of active managers seeking alpha. They tend to take on more managers than they can comfortably handle, and some managers see this as beneficial, since it tends to result in only occasional, minimal and largely uninformed monitoring. Yet what the Americans call 'dumb money' comes at a price, since any deviation, no matter how small or how short, below the agreed benchmark may well attract aggressive and disproportionate attention.

Opportunities in what to these investors will be 'new' asset types will be mainly confined to large, established players who spend heavily on PR and investor relations, not least because they will almost always be channelled through advisers, whether general consultants or specialist gatekeepers, and such third parties will always favour big brand names.

At the other end of the barbell, the new breed of ultra-sophisticated investors is likely to be pursuing a barbell strategy of its own. On the one hand, these investors will be hungry for large amounts of relevant beta in a form that is cheap and readily accessible, and possibly through a single manager who is able to offer all these exposures across the spectrum of asset types. On the other hand, they will probably also be looking for managers who can demonstrably add value in some specialist area.

In contrast to their less sophisticated brethren, they will pursue opportunities across a broad spread of asset types. Yet even as this trend develops it may start to lose much of its relevance as investors move beyond consideration of asset types completely, because it is here that we may find things such as trend investing and risk factor investing. At the larger end of the scale, these sophisticated investors are likely to pursue direct investing, which is considered below, while at the smaller end, they are the most likely to consider the 'exotics' – for example, recent offerings that have apparently sparked interest from family offices have included diamonds and Stradivarius violins.

A move to direct investing?

Another consequence of this shift to higher levels of sophistication has been a growth in the number of investors deciding to make their own investments directly, whether in firms, projects or assets. This can take one of three forms, and it may be that these are pursued in sequence as a natural series of evolution, though they can and do overlap. First, the institution starts to invest alongside its existing managers; this is generally called 'co-investment'. Second, they continue their manager relationships, though they may reduce both their number and their overall amount, and also begin direct investing; this is naturally a somewhat sensitive state of affairs, since they may well in certain cases be competing with managers with whom they have a parallel relationship, a relationship furthermore that will almost certainly entitle them to receive confidential information about the manager's affairs. Third, they may finally eschew the services of managers altogether if they have by this time built up specialist teams of sufficient size and expertise within their own organisation.

As we saw in Chapter 10, this shift has until now probably been driven largely by concern about fees and their return-destructive potential. For a large investor, the cost of employing even a highly paid team internally will almost always be significantly less than private equity or hedge fund type manager remuneration on an equivalent amount of capital.

It is possible, however, that in the years to come the shift will also become driven by other factors. One may be a desire to preserve confidentiality of information as regulation forces more and more transparency on private fund vehicles, coupled with 'headline risk' – the desire not to be named in the media in connection with a failed or controversial investment. Another may be a growing scarcity of quality investment opportunities, coupled with a reluctance by vendors to be seen to be selling to overtly 'financial' (as opposed to 'strategic') buyers. Yet another may be driven by a shift to real assets (see below). To invest indirectly, for example, in a forestry project with a 30-year investment horizon requires a great deal of faith that the manager (who will not have anything like that length of track record) will still be around in 30 years' time to manage out the investment.

Whatever the case, investment managers in many areas must be prepared to face increasing competition from a significant proportion of those whom they have been accustomed to thinking of as their clients, whether actual or potential. Some of the large Canadian pension funds have been making direct investments for some years, while many sovereign wealth funds not only make their own private equity and real estate investments, but also have in-house teams participating in infrastructure projects and pursuing hedge-fund-type programmes.

This shift towards direct investing on the part of the world's largest and most sophisticated investors may also, of course, form part of a move towards trend investing. Indeed, trend investing is as yet incapable of being exercised in any other way, since at the time of writing suitable dedicated fund vehicles do not exist. In large part this is probably a consequence of investors' obsession with categorisation. Any such vehicle would probably have to be a multi-asset type in nature and investors would struggle to fit it into their nice, cosy allocation system.

Debt and currency

These next few dynamics really belong together and, since they have already been mentioned elsewhere, can be touched on relatively lightly in closing.

Put briefly, the world is divided into monetarists and others. It is acknowledged that this is a simplistic generalisation; monetarists come in many theoretical shapes and sizes, but for the purposes of a summary a few paragraphs in length, it will suffice. Monetarists, whatever their specific shades of opinion, all share a common belief, namely that governments cannot issue more money (though precise agreement on what actually constitutes 'money' is more problematic) without causing upward pressure on prices or, to put it more plainly, inflation. Even the cautious Greg Mankiw is surprisingly unequivocal on this point. One of his famous Ten Principles is simply put as: 'Prices rise when government prints too much money'.[2]

At the time of writing (late 2012), governments around the world have effectively been printing huge amounts of money through the medium of quantitative easing (QE), a programme whereby central banks buy back the debt instruments of their own government from banks, crediting the banks electronically with credit balances in return. It is envisaged, and indeed intended, that the banks will then lend each such balance out many times over, thus creating new money which can be spent by individuals and firms in an attempt to kick-start economic growth (or, on a more cynical view, to create an illusory feel-good factor among the electorate ahead of the next election by conjuring up some phoney short-term wealth).

At the heart of the monetarist creed lies the famous equation $MV = PQ$, with PQ standing for the level of economic activity (broadly equivalent to GDP), M for money, and V for something called velocity, which is the speed with which money travels around the system, the number of times every year that the same unit of currency gets re-spent. Thus, if either the amount of money in circulation or the rate at which it gets spent increases, then so too should GDP.[3]

So far, so good. The problem comes with the right-hand side of the equation. Q stands for the quantity of goods and services that gets bought every year, and P for the price at which they are sold. Obviously, this is a somewhat abstract notion, since no accepted standardised units actually exist, certainly not any that can be applied across the whole economy, but the logic is impeccable. If such a unit of quantity could be identified and agreed upon, then clearly P could be calculated, since we know the GDP figure, which *is* reported.

However, factories cannot, when faced with greatly increased demand, just double their capacity overnight. Service businesses may well be in

---

2. Greg Mankiw, *Principles of Economics*, New York: Thomson, 2004.
3. For a fuller explanation, see Guy Fraser-Sampson, *The Mess We're In: Why Politicians Can't Solve Financial Crises*, London: Elliott & Thompson, 2012.

a similar position, since it takes time to find and train new staff. Thus, once any available slack in the system has been taken up then demand will exceed supply and prices will rise in consequence; and inflation will occur. It is only fair to state that monetarists differ among themselves as to exactly how and why this happens. The classical view has been that velocity was constant, though few today would agree with such a view. However, it may well be what economists call 'sticky' (resistant to change in the short term). Today some believe that the proposition just stated explains how inflation arises, while others go further and argue that money is not just a medium of exchange but an economic good in its own right, so that when the amount of it available increases then its perceived value (purchasing power) will fall. Whatever the case, Mankiw's principle (his ninth of ten) is generally accepted.

This raises an interesting and disturbing possibility. If the spread of government and corporate debt around the world continues unchecked, and governments compound this by continuing to pump new money and new debt into the system, might we not see a situation in which money steadily loses its value, leading to high asset price inflation for things such as energy, commodities and real estate?

There are some who question whether things might go even further, with some sort of major systemic failure as recognition spreads that paper currency has ceased to have any real value. If this seems to be an unduly alarmist thought, two facts are worth recording. First, our present experiment with paper currency unsupported by anything but politicians' promises (fiat money, to give it its technical name) has been going on only since 1971, when the post-war Bretton Woods monetary system collapsed. Second, every previous recorded attempt to introduce paper currency in countries around the world has ended in failure. The only near-exception was China, which managed to make it work in various forms for about 300 years in the early middle ages (Sung, Yuan and Ming dynasties). Other experiments, such as in Sweden in the seventeenth century and France in the eighteenth, lasted a few decades at best.

So, no matter how unlikely you may consider it to be, with governments around the world seemingly embarked on a headlong debt spree and money-printing programme, a collapse of paper currency must surely form part of any investor's scenario planning.

It is difficult to guess how such a scenario might play out, and how we might seek to protect ourselves against it as much as possible. It seems logical to assume that contagion would spread rapidly from cash outwards, affecting cash-like investments first and most seriously. Government bonds would thus be an obvious candidate to avoid, with corporate bonds and currency based fund strategies following closely behind.

What might happen to equities is more difficult to fathom. On the one hand, the world will always need commercial activity, and so owning literally a share in a business must offer the holder some real long-term value. On the other hand, if both money and the banking system were to collapse, then any normal commercial intercourse might become impossible, with no way of transferring funds electronically, and in any event (as has happened in many countries in the past) business partners being unwilling to accept even their own currency in payment. The best guess is probably that the business system would find some way to adapt and survive (at least one start-up business is already putting together a global, barter-based business exchange), if only because the alternative would be too horrible to contemplate, and would also presumably obviate the objectives of many investors in any case.

Easier to 'call' are real assets, such as real estate, energy assets, commodities and, of course, gold. If a downward spiral towards worthless paper does indeed gather pace, then expect these to gain rapidly in popularity, and thus price.

In the shorter term, one would also have to consider dealing with high levels of inflation, a topic already covered elsewhere in the book. However, unlike in earlier spells of high inflation, such as in the UK during the 1970s, it is possible that things could be much more concentrated this time around, with the period of high inflation being compacted into a short period between a relatively 'normal' rate of inflation and some sort of failure of the financial system.

In other words, seeking to avoid the effects of the policy (or maladministration, as many would now argue) of governments and central banks (which are effectively the same thing, no matter how much the latter may be dressed up as 'independent') may itself now be a viable strategic imperative if you identify such maladministration as the most pressing threat to your activities, as many investors do increasingly. However, many more clearly do not, as, like demented squirrels, they frantically stuff domestic government bonds into their own particular hollow tree. It is truly terrifying to think what might happen to investments such as pension funds if, after all, these 'squirrels' are wrong.

A shift towards real assets

While many of the world's investors seem happy to gamble everything on such events not transpiring, some of their more sophisticated brethren are way ahead of them, making significant allocations to real assets, and spreading their fixed income exposure around a number of issuers in different nations and currencies, concentrating on those that have relatively low levels of debt. One approach, for example, focuses on countries that have a relatively high proportion of foreign assets compared to foreign obligations.

A shift to real assets, though it seems indicated by any even vaguely objective view of the global fiscal and monetary situation, is, however, easier said than done and is not without risks of its own. First, there are problems with access. While some, such as physical gold, can be held through ETFs, and real estate can be held through REITs,[4] others, such as timber and agricultural land, present greater difficulty.

If held through an investment vehicle, one is taking very significant manager risk given the very long-term nature of the investment and (usually) the short-term nature of the manager's track record. Even then, it is difficult to reach the required level of diversification by geography and (in the case of timber) age and variety.

The real problem with real assets such as this, however, is political risk, though this can manifest itself in different ways.

If the proliferation and devaluation of money gathers pace, then one obvious consequence will be for governments to ban the private ownership of gold, as used to be the case in the USA. We have already seen one occurrence of this in Europe, with the Dutch government trying to outlaw the holding of gold by Dutch pension funds (apparently on the basis that it was not a proper investment, while Dutch government bonds were). Luckily, while the Dutch government won initially, they lost subsequently on appeal, but do not expect that to be the end of the story. There is no point in a government debauching its currency unless they can force people to hold and use it while they do so.

Real estate, being a fixed asset, is a soft target for both taxation and confiscation. We are already seeing moves in various countries in Europe to impose property taxes on perceived 'luxury' residences (the stated target in London would embrace many ordinary two-bedroom flats). There seems no reason why, if the public finances are finally buckling under the strain, that similar measures might not be extended to commercial and industrial properties.

In fact, it is this inability to move them away of the control of rogue government action that is the main drawback to these sorts of real assets. For example, the Brazilian government has revived legislation severely restricting the foreign ownership of land. So, yes, real assets offer a good theoretical hedge against financial suicide by governments, but be aware that they may carry significant risks of their own in practice.

---

4. But check this. In some places, notably in the UK, REITs are often operating businesses in such areas as property development or even investment management.

Conclusion

It is both difficult and dangerous to attempt to predict the future. The above musings are not intended as firm projections of what will actually occur (and even if they were, the timing would remain uncertain). They are instead offered as food for thought during discussions of scenario planning, and the threats and opportunities that may be present within the environment, whether actually or potentially, but as yet unsuspected.

As we draw towards the end of the book there may be some who feel cheated by having bought a book on investment strategy that does not set out flowcharts and checklists, depicting a perfect professional process for bringing order out of chaos. Sadly, real life does not operate like that, and to be fair such aids are largely used in business schools for teaching purposes, and then only with the very heavy caveat that they demonstrate the theory but provide only a basic guideline for what is likely to happen in theory.

In practice, investment organisations are bedevilled by strong individuals at senior levels who tend to have both large egos and narrow minds, a combination that both discourages discussion and mistrusts new ideas. They are likely to find their perfect foil in colleagues who rejoice in being told what to do, whether internally or by regulators, who are obsessed with tactical and operational detail, and see any attempt at strategic level thought as being likely to introduce dangerous amounts of uncertainty into their cosy view of the world.

In practice, then, investment strategy is likely in many cases to be the art of the possible rather than the desirable or optimal, and unless we recognise this from the outset we are likely to end up frustrated and disappointed. The sad truth is that many people simply do not want to think about things, still less to make decisions or take independent action, and it is these people who are often promoted to senior positions precisely because they are seen as 'a safe pair of hands'. It is almost certainly for this reason that the portfolios of most investors look suspiciously alike, as do the offerings of most investment managers.

For the latter at least, realisation is finally starting to dawn that being a 'me too' player in a world that is both increasingly competitive and increasingly suspicious of alpha return-seeking is not a very desirable thing to be after all, and that far from avoiding survival risk it may actually increase it dramatically. The problem they are facing is that, not having ever put in place a proper strategic process, they are left with a growing awareness that they need to do things differently, but with no process for determining how. There is in fact a deliberate mistake in that last sentence: because they have no strategic process in place they do not even understand that most of the time they do not need to do things differently, but rather to do different things.

For the former, there seems less of a prospect of change because of the dead hands of regulators and politicians on the tiller. On the one hand, many investors are increasingly restricted in their choice of types of investment (which, in one view, will continue to narrow until it permits only bonds issued by the domestic government, where this is not already the case). On the other, they are excused from having to take responsibility for their actions so that no real sanction is visited on them should they, for example, manage their pension scheme into a significant funding deficit. Small wonder that so many of the world's investors adopt the style of 'Pierre' rather than 'Maria'.

So do not go into an investment organisation expecting them to think as you do, or even necessarily to think at all in any real strategic sense about what they are doing. The best you can do is to seek to nibble around the edges. Quite often, the best way of doing this is to appeal to practical concerns, which might at least gain the sympathy of some of your introverted/conscientious colleagues. Is it really sensible, for example, to seek to have so many managers when the time of your committee is so limited? If you find such a question starting to gain traction, you may be able to use it as a Trojan horse to gain access to such issues as choosing between active and passive investing.

For a lucky few, however, those who will increasingly be at one end of the barbell described earlier, you will find yourself among kindred spirits who are genuinely interested in analysing and discussing not only the investment environment as a whole but also the needs of the organisation, and how the two might best be reconciled. It is people like these to whom this book is dedicated and at whom it is aimed.

For them, it will I hope point up the sorts of stages such a discussion might go through and the sorts of issues that will be discussed. It is not intended as a universal practical handbook, for such a thing is almost certainly impossible. Nor does it assume any measure of infallibility. How could it? We are dealing with concepts, judgements and instincts, precisely the sorts of things that the world of finance and investment usually refuses to take into consideration precisely because they recognise and embrace uncertainty.

What it *does* aim to do is very simple. To make people think. To make them aware that the strategic process is not some add-on luxury that might be indulged in at some time in the future as a pleasant afternoon's diversion, but an essential starting point. That any action or decision taken except within the framework of a broader strategic plan is almost certainly an action or decision wasted, and perhaps even actively harmful to what you *should* be trying to achieve. Above all, to learn to recognise the dire affect of groupthink, and to challenge it.

We began with some Second World War generals, so let us end with another. General Patton once said: 'If everyone is thinking the same, then somebody isn't thinking.'

Index

Printed and bound by CPI Group (UK) Ltd, Croydon, CR0 4YY